CW00498529

# Melton - a changing village

*by* Robert Blake

©*Robert Blake* 1994
*Printed by Technographic, Brightlingsea, Essex*
*Design and layout by SOS Design, Ardleigh, Essex*

This book is

dedicated to

Meltonians both

past and present

and all those who

love and appreciate

the traditional values

of village life.

# Contents

# Acknowledgements

My thanks to all the friends who have helped with the preparation of this book; to Liz Emsley for the typing of the text and Margaret Hughes for producing the maps of Melton and assisting with proof reading.

I am indebted to those Meltonians who have responded in encouraging and directing me to the most salient issues facing our village. Over the years I have listened not only to the views and opinions of the older members of our community but also to those who only recently came to live here. In addition I have found the approach and views of the children and young people, who are uninhibited by bias or tradition, most refreshing and direct.

A special debt is owed to my wife, who as Parish Recorder for Melton has encouraged and supported me in this work.

My thanks to Lance Cooper for his expertise and advice on photographic matters.

*Robert Blake*

*Other publications by Robert Blake:*

Mrs Parsley Remembers: In the Shadow of the Big House

Woodbridge and its Environs

Defection, Why? *a survey by Robert Blake and Sheila Jefferson into why volunteers volunteer, and also leave charitable agencies.*

The following books have been most helpful in the preparation of this work:

*Cecil Bentham:*
Melton and its Churches
(East Anglian Magazine 1981)

*Peter Bishop:*
Grundisburgh: The History of a Suffolk Village
(Silent Books 1992)

*Ronald Blythe:*
Akenfield
(Penguin Press 1969)

*Rosie Caulfield:*
Suffolk Gems
(Hamler Publishing 1993)

*Peggy Cole:*
A Country Girl at Heart
(Brechinset Publications 1985)

*George Ewart Evans:*
All his many books considering country life and the oral tradition

*Paul Jennings:*
The Living Village
(Hodder & Stoughton 1968)

*Wallace Morfey:*
Painting the Day
(Boydell Press 1986)

*Roland Parker:*
The Common Stream
(Paladin Press 1976)

*Robert Semper:*
Woodbridge and Beyond
(East Anglian Magazine 1972)

*John Hadfield (editor):*
The Shell Book of English Villages
(Peerage Books 1980)

# Preface

The infinite beauty and variety of Suffolk villages is well known, as is the steady and sturdy quality of their inhabitants. It is not long since their horizon was limited by the range of the horse; their needs met by local craftsmen. Even today the village person differs from townsmen (and women) in many ways; yet these are surely becoming rarer under urban pressures and modern mobility – with improved communication. Robert Blake knows this, and is eager to seek authentic glimpses of the older way of life – when transport was difficult, electricity still in the distant future, television unknown, village inhabitants and their extended families stayed for generations in the same area.

He does this by contrasting and comparing contemporary life in his Suffolk home of Melton – once a true village, then a posting station on the turnpike to the east coast ports, and now virtually a suburb of Woodbridge – with patterns of past days.

Do thou, reader, likewise. Yet Suffolk remains Old England to this day; long let her remain so.

*His Honour Bertrand Richards*

*Melton Hall*

**Melton Hall, Summer 1908**

**A fine Regency house built on the site of a much earlier dwelling that was destroyed by fire**

# Melton - White's appraisal of 1855

"Melton is a large, pleasant and well-built village, on the western side of the river Deben, about a mile north-east of Woodbridge. Its parish increased its population from 501 in 1801 to 1039 in 1851, including 269 in Suffolk Lunatic Asylum. It comprises about 1,410 acres of land stretching southward to the suburbs of Woodbridge – from which the navigation of the Deben has been extended up to a quay which was constructed some 15 years ago (1840).

The land belongs chiefly to Capt. Aplin, C. Walford, Mrs. Buckingham, Mrs. Bland, E. Jenny, T. Pytches, and J. Jeaffreson Esqrs., and a few smaller owners. Foxburgh Hall, the beautiful seat of Charles Walford, Esq., stands on a commanding eminence in the midst of tasteful pleasure grounds. Melton Lodge, the seat of Capt. Aplin, has a beautiful park extending over 48 acres. There are several other neat mansions in the parish, and also a large iron foundry and machine works.

The Dean and Chapter of Ely are lords of the manor and patrons of the Church (St. Andrew and St. Etheldreda) which is an ancient structure, standing in a large burial ground, a mile from the village.

The National School was built in 1845 at the cost of £250. Wilford Bridge, which crosses the Deben near Melton, was rebuilt in 1539.

Suffolk Lunatic Asylum, which stands in a healthy and airy situation within the parish boundaries, was originally erected as a House of Industry for the maintenance of the poor but in 1827 the building was purchased by the County Magistrates, chiefly for the reception of pauper lunatics. There are now some 260 patients labouring under the worst of human maladies - insanity.

**Melton Old Church and surrounding countryside, photographed in 1994**

This useful and well-regulated establishment, including the purchase of the grounds and the original buildings, and the subsequent alterations, enlargements and improvements, with the furniture etc. had cost about £30,000 in 1844, but since that year the asylum has been considerably enlarged and improved."

*Taken from White's Suffolk Directory, 1855.*

# *Introduction*

The question of whether Melton should be considered a "village proper" or a suburb of Woodbridge is not new. Nearly sixty years ago the Suffolk Mercury wrote: "Melton is regarded by a great number of people to be a kind of suburb to Woodbridge, and in view of the manner in which the two places virtually merge... there is some excuse for such a belief." At the outset it must be stated categorically that under no circumstances can Melton be described as a conventional or beautiful village, there being no central green with church, public house and pretty cottages around its periphery. The village follows the main road from Woodbridge through to Wickham Market and is crossed by roads and lanes from Hasketon, Bredfield, Ufford and Sutton. The River Deben, although once of some beauty, is now overshadowed by commercial and light industrial buildings and its new wall appears as a visual barrier. The railway line from Ipswich to Lowestoft forms a further cut to the village. However, gems remain to be discovered. There are enjoyable walks along lanes and footpaths, many offering glimpses of the Deben and beyond, but also an opportunity to forget much of the twentieth century development within the parish boundaries. The Old Church, nestling on the borders with Ufford, the watermill and Roman decoys, are only to be found by the diligent explorer. Larger mansions and houses, many of which afford excellent views over the Deben, are set in secluded locations, only visible to those on foot. Cottages and old farmhouses are now obscured or "lost" amidst post-war housing developments*. Other "peculiars" also worthy of discovery include for example the First World War air-raid shelter behind William Marjoram's "Castle Cote", the remains of a mausoleum in the garden of "The Retreat" or the site of Melton's famous spring. In a similar way, St Andrew's new Church, although having an austere exterior, possesses one of the few remaining pre-Reformation seven sacrament fonts. The Coach and Horses and Horse and Groom public houses not only have a wealth of ancient timbers but also stories worth including here.

In the following pages I look at Melton both past and present from several viewpoints, contrasting and comparing in order to come to a clearer conclusion of the true status of Melton at the turn of the twenty-first century. I make no apology for the bias towards inhabitants because it has been, and is still, true that the people in the locality give the character to any place. As far as possible, those involved in Melton life are speaking for themselves, and I have been very fortunate in having the support and enthusiasm of many present-day Meltonians. This has been achieved by interviews and written contributions. I have had access to many previously unpublished accounts of events and personalities involved in Parish life. By allowing a free rein to contributors, a happy variation in presentation is to be found, though some repetition is inevitable. Personal opinions may at times be at variance with the general thesis of this book but, intentionally, I have not influenced or edited these, and include them as expressed by those contributing to this work. I have not pursued some of the questions raised both within the general text and by contributors unless I feel that they are relevant to the general theme of this book.

One of the most common myths of history, and particularly when listening to those reminiscing about the past, is to view life as a static unmoving picture. However, this is not substantiated. Real "Cranfords" never existed, and village life has continually changed and developed, partly as a result of social and economic changes but also spurred on by participating local characters finding themselves in the right place at the right time. Any cursory study of Melton over the last 150 years confirms this. For instance, large businesses and major employers of local labour have come and gone. Page and Girling's Foundry, Melton Docks, Bilby's building "empire" and even St Audry's Hospital are now all part of history. The developments in the post-war period have been even more radical and have changed the whole village more in half a century than in the previous thousand years. I have carefully introduced and given emphasis to this when approaching the central question and thrust of this book - Melton's status.

Social changes have affected Melton as with other parts of rural Suffolk. In one respect because Melton had no Lord of the

* see Domesday Survey 1986, Appendix 4

Manor or a single large landowner, having instead a "number of neat and pleasant mansions", whose owners competed in a local hierarchy, this allowed villagers to shift and change allegiance over the years. The dependence upon agriculture became increasingly indirect with the development of associated trades and industries from the seventeenth century. St Audry's, on the periphery of the village offered a major source of employment, and gave independence to many local people. Woodbridge, immediately to the south of Melton, likewise offered employment and from an early time, even when the village remained virtually self-supporting, gave competition to Melton businesses.

A consensus from those involved in many aspects of Melton life is that the community remains alive and vibrant, and this is confirmed not only by those contributing personally to this book, but also by the directory of organisations operating within the village (Appendix 1). At the outset however, it can be claimed that those persons and organisations only involve a very small minority of the population. People who are active in local affairs tend to share their enthusiasms and it should be no surprise that many "wear hats which are frequently changed". For the vast majority their residence within the village boundary has no particular relevance; they look outside for their economic and social welfare, making no practical contribution to the life of Melton. This, sadly, has been confirmed by the questionnaire (Appendix 2) which was distributed to virtually every house (over 1,400) within Melton boundaries, offering confidentiality, anonymity and the opportunity to voice any concern about life in the village. However, the small number of replies not only confirms the low sense of corporate identity but also a general malaise towards Melton's affairs particularly from those living in the large housing estates. This is proving difficult to overcome even by the great enthusiasm of those committed and involved in village activities.

**Aerial photograph looking north, 1994**

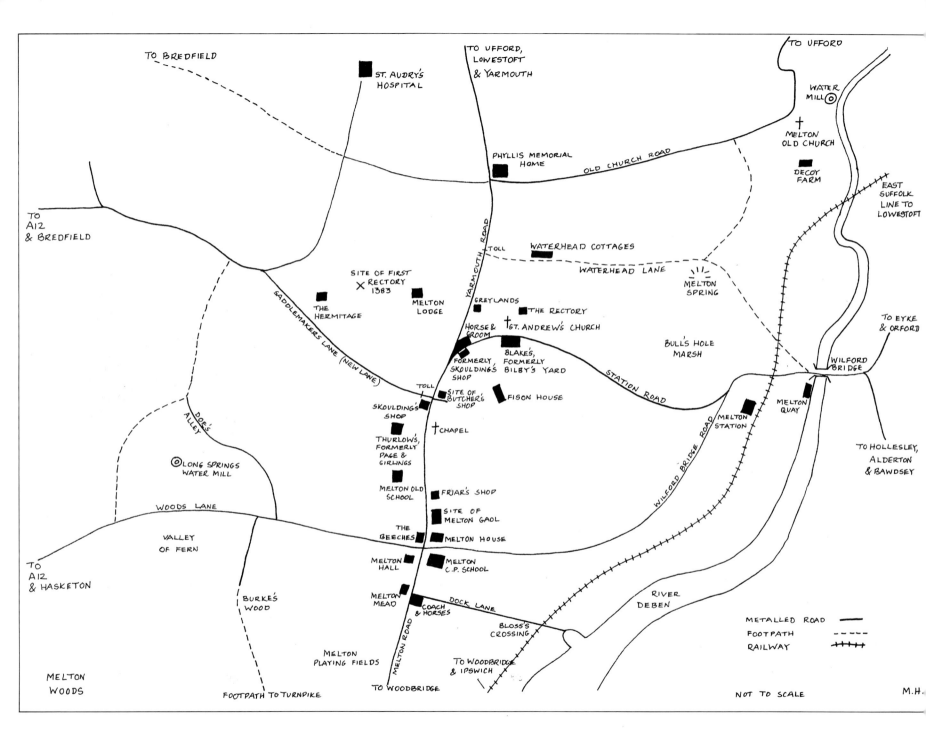

TO BREDFIELD

TO UFFORD,
LOWESTOFT
& YARMOUTH

TO UFFORD

ST. AUDRY'S
HOSPITAL

WATER
MILL ⊙

MELTON
OLD CHURCH

PHYLLIS MEMORIAL
HOME

OLD CHURCH ROAD

DECOY
FARM

EAST
SUFFOLK
LINE TO
LOWESTOFT

TO
A12
& BREDFIELD

YARMOUTH ROAD

TOLL

WATERHEAD COTTAGES

WATERHEAD LANE

MELTON
SPRING

SADDLEMAKERS LANE (NEW LANE)

SITE OF FIRST
RECTORY 1383

THE
HERMITAGE

MELTON
LODGE

GREYLANDS

THE RECTORY

HORSE &
GROOM

† ST. ANDREW'S CHURCH

BULL'S HOLE
MARSH

TO EYKE
& ORFORD

BLAKE'S,
FORMERLY
BILBY'S YARD

STATION ROAD

WILFORD
BRIDGE

FORMERLY
SKOULDING'S
SHOP

TOLL

SITE OF
BUTCHER'S
SHOP

FISON HOUSE

WILFORD BRIDGE ROAD

MELTON
STATION

MELTON
QUAY

MELTON
QUAY

DOE'S
ALLEY

SKOULDING'S
SHOP

† CHAPEL

TO HOLLESLEY,
ALDERTON
& BAWDSEY

LONG SPRINGS
WATER MILL ⊙

THURLOW'S,
FORMERLY
PAGE &
GIRLINGS

WOODS LANE

MELTON OLD
SCHOOL

FRIAR'S SHOP

VALLEY
OF FERN

SITE OF
MELTON GAOL

RIVER
DEBEN

THE
BEECHES

MELTON HOUSE

TO
A12
& HASKETON

MELTON
HALL

MELTON
C.P. SCHOOL

BURKE'S
WOOD

MELTON
MEAD

COACH
& HORSES

DOCK LANE

METALLED ROAD
FOOTPATH
RAILWAY

MELTON ROAD

BLOSS'S
CROSSING

MELTON
PLAYING FIELDS

TO WOODBRIDGE
& IPSWICH

MELTON
WOODS

FOOTPATH TO TURNPIKE

TO WOODBRIDGE

NOT TO SCALE

M.H.

3   **Melton 1994, showing landmarks and principle transport routes**

# Development of the Village

There is often speculation as to why the old Church is so far out of the Village, and it is commonly thought that it was the Black Death in the 14th Century that caused the Village to move away from its original position. However, although there are deaths recorded, they were not in sufficient numbers to account for the move.

Melton, or Meltuna as it was called in the Middle Ages, was a Settlement or a Hamlet, with Roman and Saxon origins. There would have been a wooden Church run by Monks, a water mill, and decoy farm, with a small collection of cottages, and a crossing of the Deben at Wilford.

A Roman kiln was found, with tiles in place, in 1846, and a Saxon Amulet was discovered some thirty years later during vault digging in the Churchyard. The Mill and Decoy Farm are mentioned in Domesday Book; the Church, dedicated to St. Etheldreda and St. Andrew, belonged to the Abbot of Ely and formed part of Etheldreda's Hundreds, and, in the opinion of the historian Norman Scarfe, a Church has stood on the site from that time.

**Melton Old Mill, c1850**

**Melton Old Church
by Isaac Johnson, c1800**

The first recorded Rector was Theodwine in 1147 and from then on the list of Priests serving Melton continues to the present day. The notable features of the Church are the rare triple Brass depicting a Priest and his parents, dated 1436 (the Brass is unusual, in that the Priest appears in academic costume, wearing the hood of his Degree, not as Priests were generally shown, wearing Mass Vestments) and the Font, now in the new Church, which is 15th Century and is one of only 38 in England with carvings of the pre-Reformation Seven Sacraments. With the addition of the Tower in 1440, they are suggestive of considerable wealth in Melton at that time and indicate that the Church was no mere wayside Chapel. There were four Bells: one, engraved "Miles Graye made Me" in 1618, is still in the old Church, the other three were moved to the new Church.

The opening up of the country by the Turnpike roads and travel by Stage Coach made it impossible to use some of the old

**Tollgate cottage at Yarmouth Road**

roads. The London to Yarmouth (South Town) was one of the main Highways through Melton and the road leading to the Church was impassable to Coaches, so the road to Wickham Market out of the Village was straightened, leaving the Church isolated in its peaceful surroundings.

Melton, being strategically placed, became an important route centre. Trades sprang up along the Turnpike road, blacksmiths, wheelwrights, travellers' rests, general provision and specialists' shops, etc. The Coach and Horses served as a major Staging Post, providing both accommodation and change of horses. The main roads, however suffered from the increasing traffic and villages on the routes complained about the cost of upkeep, so in 1799 an Act of Parliament was passed to allow Toll Gates to be set at entrances to affected villages. Cottages were built for the Gate keepers who collected the Tolls before lifting the bar to give passage. Melton had three such Gates, one at the top of Wood's Lane, one at Saddlemakers Lane (previously New Road) and the third on the Wickham Market road. There was, however, no Toll Gate from Wilford Bridge, although this was the first possible crossing of

**Tollgate ticket, May 25, 1787**

the river. There was no significant trade from the other side as the land, compared with the hinterland, was comparatively poor and unproductive and as a result the whole area was less populated.

Richard Cook left £20 in his Will of 1539, together with two other Legacies for repairing the bridge when the authorities would undertake it (i.e. the first bridge at Wilford must therefore significantly pre-date 1539). That bridge stood until 1764 when it was pulled down and rebuilt with brick. However, this bridge was replaced in 1798 by one built of white brick and stone. It was the floods of 1939 that finally finished the old bridge when the foundations were washed away and it became unsafe. A new single span bridge was built and the road straightened, as, with the development of the American Air Bases for the 1939-45 War, a wider straighter crossing of the River became imperative.

In the mid-seventeenth century, the banking of the river as far as Melton brought great changes to the area. Before that, the low-lying land would have flooded with each incoming tide, but as the marshes drained and dried, houses and cottages spread towards the river and Wilford Bridge, and the centre of the Village gradually moved and grew. With the building of the Dock in 1793 river trade expanded and a Quay was built in 1840. The coming of the Ipswich to Lowestoft railway line in 1859, with the large goods yard and station at Melton, was an important development which brought more trade to the village.

**Tollgate cottage at Wood's Lane, demolished in the mid-1930s**

Whereas Woodbridge had the wealthy Augustinian Foundation to foster the growth of the Town, Melton had no Religious Houses, and when the County Sessions were moved to Woodbridge by Thomas Seckford in 1575, Melton lost prestige and had to rely on trade for prosperity.

The Church continued to serve the people, but as the Village grew, because of its size accommodation became a problem and from 1800 onwards proposals were put forward for enlargement: A Gallery was built in the Tower for the "minstrels" and the Chancel taken down to allow extra seating. A suggestion to build a side aisle was rejected by the Charity Commissioners, so finally in 1865 it was decided to build a new, larger Church in a more central position in the Village and to convert the old Church into a Cemetery Chapel. It was a momentous decision for the Village to make.

The arrival of motor transport meant that the horse drawn hearse was superseded and funeral services could be held in the new Parish Church, so the uses of the old Church declined further until it was declared redundant in 1977. A proposal was made to sell the old Church for residential purposes, but local people rejected it, for many generations of Melton families had worshipped there and were buried in the churchyard and the

**Accident on Wilford Bridge, 1939**

Church was considered an essential part of the Village heritage.

In 1982 the Melton Old Church Society was formed to care for and maintain the building for use as a Christian Community and Educational Centre, where lectures, concerts etc. could be held. Thus the old Church regained a position in the Parish and stands in its beautiful surroundings as a link with the past, yet looking to the future with confidence.

There has been and remains a long tradition of East Anglian artists coming to Melton and district, not only because of the local countryside but particularly with the outstanding views over the Deben. Notable was Thomas Churchyard (often known as the poor man's lawyer because of his recognised social conscience). His family farmed extensively in the area, and his father Jonathan was Melton's butcher. For many years Thomas Churchyard and his family lived at The Beeches, Melton, and some of his best work dates to this period. Both Thomas and his wife are buried in the Old Church graveyard.

Major Edmund Van Someren, the well-known artist, whose forte was portrait painting, came to Melton soon after the First World War in order to recover from the traumas he had suffered. For the remaining 40 years of his life, he and his wife enjoyed the peace and tranquillity of Melton, and he is remembered with love and respect both as a kind and dignified man and as an accomplished artist. The Van Somerens lie in the quiet of the old churchyard, a mere twenty yards from the grave of Thomas Churchyard and his wife.

**River Deben and Wilford Bridge c1900, photograph by W. H. Needs**

7    **Melton Quay, 1904**

# Trade & Industry

Melton's prosperity, as has been noted earlier, was based upon trade. Industries grew up in the village largely as a result of Melton's strategic position and also its growing importance over the centuries as a route centre. Trade passed through the village from the Deben, steadily increasing with the construction of Melton Docks and the quay near to Wilford Bridge. An improved road system brought more transport and associated trades. From 1859 the Great Eastern Railway, with its station and large goods yard at Melton, ensured that both freight and passengers passed through the village. Industries sprang up served by improved transport facilities. The required labour force materialised; from the late eighteenth century increasing numbers of cottages and houses were constructed and, not surprisingly, the population rose steadily.

Added to these on-going advantageous factors, the natural beauty of the area, with its fertile soil and rich woodlands with views of the Deben, led to many "neat mansions"* being built in selected sites. These in turn required labour and meant increased opportunities for employment. St Audry's was another major employer from the mid-nineteenth century. Melton's industrial base was broad and diverse enough to sustain steady development for the last two hundred years. An elderly resident recently listed the number of semi-skilled and unskilled women employed (non residential employment) in the inter-war years. She estimated these to be over 200, and she included St Audry's (65), the laundry (45), the school kitchens (5), shops (10 to 15), with more than 30 houses employing part-time domestic staff, ranging from "common chars" to cooks and those enjoying more sophisticated titles!

Male employment in the village was significant. Agriculture was labour intensive until after the second World War (and Melton's increasing agricultural loss to residential building did not affect this traditional employment base until the construction of the Hall Farm Road and St Andrew's estates in the 1950s and '60s). The foundry in its heyday employed well over 100 men, and Bilby's, the builders, offered employment for more than half this number. Those working on the docks, quay and Great Eastern station and goods yard would be in three figures. Added to these, associated trades and smaller employers (not forgetting St Audry's) would mean that a total of well over 1,000 men worked within the village boundaries at the turn of the century.

Any comparison with the late 1990s is difficult to assess accurately. Improved mobility means that the average person will travel beyond walking distance to his or her place of work. Modern industrial units require highly skilled labour and tend to employ smaller numbers – further, the turnover of both labour and the smaller businesses themselves tends to be high – some will expand and move to larger premises while others cease to operate after a relatively short period. There are some 25 custom built industrial units, many sited unobtrusively and screened from the main roads. We estimate there are between 50 and 65 employers in Melton overall, with perhaps 250-280 employees (excluding domestic work). Our research indicates that less than 15% of Meltonians (male and female) in both full and part-time employment work within the village. The contemporary commercial scene, while remaining healthily based in Melton, is more diverse than in the past. Its relationship to the village (and vice versa) is difficult to assess. Location is more a question of meeting planning criteria than any traditional advantages.

**Bilby's Cottages at foot of Gallows (or Hollows) Hill from an early 20thC photograph**

* phrasing as used by William White in his famed 19thC Suffolk Directories

## Shops & Shopkeepers

**Bill of sale from Friar's**

In the early post-Second World War period Ben Friar's Pork Butchery and General Store - "The Shop, Melton"- was a thriving business, serving not only the immediate locality but delivering to a radius of more than ten miles encompassing Bromeswell, Eyke, Rendlesham, Butley, Boyton, Hollesley, Alderton, Bawdsey, Ramsholt, Shottisham, Sutton, Ufford, Bredfield, Boulge, Debach, Dallinghoo, Pettistree, Hasketon, Burgh, Grundisburgh, Bealings, Martlesham and also Woodbridge Town! Later their mobile shop was on the road for six days every week, giving customers additional choice but with the traditional Friar's assured quality. "Ben Friar generated energy and enthusiasm… and he was greatly respected by all." Stories of his quest to meet customers' requests are legendary (and not just to satisfy his more important or larger customers). Many times he would run (he never walked!) to cut a fresh lettuce or gather other produce from the market garden behind his shop for a waiting customer, or make a special trip to Ipswich for an individual item. "Open All Hours" – he was known to open up for a packet of cigarettes at 10.30 p.m. or to make a delivery to an ill or old customer who required a special delicacy. No wonder his shop was rarely empty.

Ben's personality was such that he kept together his team of six to eight full-time and several additional part-timers, many of whom worked for him and his family for over thirty years. Loyalty to customers was also assured. "Not maybe the cheapest, but the best" was his motto. Credit was another important aspect of his service and, being genuinely concerned and caring for those forced on bad times, very rarely would he resort to prosecution for non-payment. However, for his family, life could not always have been easy, as he expected the same energetic input from them and his staff as he himself gave to the business.

Christmas was always particularly demanding, with large orders to be made up and delivered. More than 200 chickens, often nearly the same number of turkeys, without considering ducks, geese and pheasants, all to be killed and dressed on the premises. Some 12-14 pigs alone would be slaughtered for the Christmas trade,

**Ben Friar with his delivery van**

**En route for Friar's slaughterhouse!**

and Friar's famous hams, sausages, all part of their renowned pork butchery, had to be carefully prepared. The second asset to the business (after its owner) was the shop's location, with its large area of land behind. This allowed abundant storage and adequate premises for their abattoir and smoke-house. The market garden fed with manure from their own pigs and hens (themselves having a diet supplemented from shop surpluses) was another important back-up. Only food in peak condition was offered for sale; to sell near or beyond the 'sell-by date' was unheard of. Although in its heyday Friar's shop revolved around Ben Friar, he was, in fact, the second generation to serve the grocery needs of the area. His father, the first James Herbert, was something of a 'wheeler-dealer' and made the shop his base for his multifarious activities. The shop, despite its diminutive size, quickly grew in turnover and, with the able assistance of his two sons Dudley and Ben (the second James Herbert), established a reputation for quality and good service. The larger and much longer established "Skouldings High Class Provision Suppliers" (later Skoulding and Felgate, and Skoulding and Tyson) stood

Thomas Churchyard's father, Jonathan, owned a butcher's shop on this site, later demolished for the entrance to Fison House

**Skoulding's premises on the corner of Station Road**

on the corner of Station Road now occupied by the Golden Grenadier Fish and Chip Shop, but these premises being 'landlocked' at that time offered poor access for delivery and limited storage facilities. Thus from the outset Friar's shop had inbuilt advantages. These became particularly evident during the war years when the business benefited from its large degree of self-sufficiency and processing of home produce. The advantages of bulk-buying allowed extras to be passed on to regular coupon-holding customers, which ensured their loyalty.

It was in the nineteen-fifties and sixties that serious competition began to be felt, partly from supermarkets but also from the Post Office bakery next door, which with the demise of its bakehouse began to sell groceries. Increased health regulations resulted first in the smokehouse being closed in 1948, and some 16 years later Friar's abattoir ceased to function. The cumulative effect was loss of independence and range of merchandise available. Overheads began to escalate, a new generation of customers more 'fickle' came 'on-stream' and parking in Melton Street despite the demolition of the old gaol, whose site provided a car park, was a major problem. Sadly the business survived less than twenty years after Ben's death and finally closed in 1982.

**Former shops in the street**

As the end of the twentieth century approaches there are only some three retail shops still open for business. These, with other service outlets, when compared with the extract from White's 1874 Suffolk Directory (Appendix 3) clearly show the decline in the number and range of both merchandise and services on offer in Melton since that time. Gone is the sweet shop at The Bowery, beloved by children at the turn of the century, and affectionately recalled by the late Bob Daines, as also are the butchers' shops, together with a whole range of smaller shops in the street, only now recorded by their former shop windows (awaiting possible future removal). The harness-makers, blacksmiths, bicycle shop and Bilby's butchers, as with Friar's shop, all went within living memory. Barry Skoulding and his sister continue to keep their family name alive in Melton as newsagents, stationers, confectioners, with the back-up of some groceries (plus the all-important reliable service of newspaper delivery to Melton and beyond). The "Golden Grenadier", occupying premises formerly of Alfred and later his son Maxwell Skoulding, offers delicious take-away food.

In the centre of Melton Street Mr Hutt now enters his second decade as Melton Postmaster and Grocer. He offers a selection of more than 2,500 items for sale, ranging from haberdashery and off licence, to fresh vegetables and produce, plus Post Office services. The shop, like its adjacent predecessor (Friar's), is open for long hours*. In many respects the range of merchandise and services are an asset as well as a liability, stock control and quality control being no mean achievement. The long opening hours are a necessity if the business is not only to survive but also flourish. The present Postmaster and grocer (wearing not just two but several hats!) has a working week often exceeding 80 hours and has taken no holiday for the past eleven years. Another major reason for the continued functioning of Melton's Post Office stores while others in the area have closed is because its proprietor has immersed himself in village life. He personally cares for Meltonians and their needs, and through his business offers his customers (both regular and not-so-regular) free grocery delivery plus excellent service.

As parish councillor he is ideally placed to reflect and represent the needs and concerns of the village. The Post Office stores with its friendly staff (currently made up of 5 part-timers) is a natural meeting point for a cross-section of the community and at all times aims to present a cheerful, welcoming place. The somewhat cramped venue is more than compensated for by the good atmosphere and, without doubt, the Post Office services (and grocery plus) are mutually compatible with each other. It has been claimed by many locals that not only is the Post Office more efficient than the service on offer in Woodbridge, but that with the range of goods available visits outside Melton are unnecessary. Certainly choice and quality are on offer and value is often there if consideration of the costs involved in travelling to Woodbridge or beyond is taken into account.

Melton's population of some 4,500 could not logically support more retail outlets than are at present provided. Each survives because of the personality of its proprietors and staff together with the goods on offer and the specialist service provided. In the past the number of shops was much greater but overheads were far lower and in many cases these businesses were run as a supplement to an already established family income.

★   Melton Post Office stores opening hours
    8.30 am - 6 pm  Monday-Wednesday
    8 30 am - 9 pm  Thursday-Friday
    8.30 am - 12 noon Saturdays
    10.00 am - 1 pm  Sundays

The village Post Office at Milestone Cottage,
c1905 (above) and 1911 (right)

## Melton Brewery

Robert Simper, in his books "The Suffolk Sandlings" and "Woodbridge and Beyond", gives credit to Sir Cuthbert Quilter of Bawdsey for opening a 'pure beer' brewery on the Coach and Horses site. Quilter was a leading advocate and supporter of 'pure beer'. As local M.P. he sponsored a campaign to introduce a 'Pure Beer Act'. Perhaps his true motives were more diverse, as he was a self-made millionaire and, saliently, two of the local county families – Tollemaches and Cobbolds – both had breweries and public houses in Suffolk. Did Quilter think of emulating them under the 'pure beer' banner? If so, he was thwarted on both counts. The 'Pure Beer Act' did not reach the Statute Book, and his venture in brewing was short lived. Local tradition maintains that the Coach and Horses brewery predates Quilter's entrepreneurial intervention by some 25 to 30 years* and it was certainly well established before the 1880s.

Brewing at the Coach and Horses was first mentioned in 1868 when John Mallett was the occupier. In 1874 Mallett is described as a brewer's agent and victualler at the Coach and Horses with Edward Smith as a brewer's assistant. For the period 1885-88 Mrs Betsy Mallett is listed as victualler and brewer's agent in residence, with Edward Smith having been promoted to brewer's manager by 1885 and to brewer by 1888. By 1892 the Malletts had left the Coach and Horses Brewery as it was now styled, and Edward Smith appears to have been in sole charge. Brewing under Edward Smith continued until 1902 when the style was changed to the Melton Brewery Company, and under this name the business remained until about 1910 when brewing ceased.

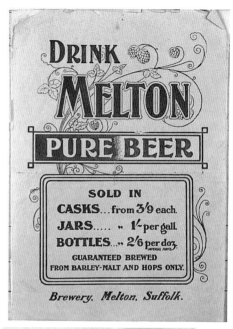

Advert for
Melton 'Pure Beer'

**Melton 'Pure Beer' bottle**

**Picture Postcard of the Melton Brewery, dated 4th March, 1908**

---

* Bottle collectors highly prize Melton Brewery bottles with rounded ends circa 1840-50.

Staff of the Maltings at the top of Melton Hill, 1905

Accident at the Coach & Horses 1932

Horse & Groom public house

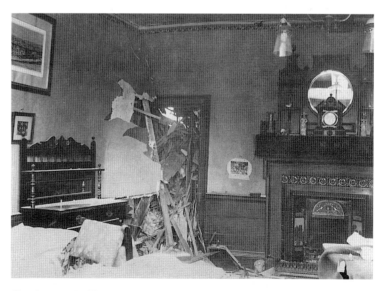

The damage inside

# The Last Blacksmith

Jack Blake died early in 1993 in his ninety-first year. Until a few months before his death he was working in his blacksmith shop opposite St. Andrew's Church. In many respects my father was a character and I am indebted to Peggy Cole for her appraisal of him.

As a family our arrival in Melton was very much the result of chance, as was our long stay in Station Road. In the early years my father only used the yard as a base (and this was his chief reason for purchasing the property in 1947), spending 95% of his time either as a threshing machine contractor working on nearby farms, or attending to agricultural machinery breakdowns away from home. During the 1950s when combine harvesters became the norm and the threshing business died away, my father continually had plans to start a new life either in Australia or Canada. There was much talk but little real action and gradually, as the blacksmith business built up, he (and we) became more settled and content to live in the village.

The location of the blacksmithy has never been ideal. For forty-five years the task of manoeuvring large machinery, notably in the early days steam engines, towing threshing machines, with 'hullers' and 'pitchers', and more recently, combine harvesters, articulated timber carriers from the Forestry Commission and four-wheel farm trailers, many of which are now more than thirty-five feet in length, was no mean feat. Great patience was (and is) required from the travellers held up in traffic jams and even more skill from those attempting to reverse between narrow gate posts into what was (and still is!) a very cluttered yard.

The range of buildings dates back to the sixteenth century, and throughout the nineteenth and early twentieth Messrs. Bilby had carried on a thriving business as builders and undertakers here. At its height there were over 100 employees, whose skills ranged through blacksmithy, carpentry, wheelwrights, undertakers, glaziers and painters. Anvil Cottage, with its fine timber frame, gable-end and Essex boarded walls, was, in Tudor times, originally a cottage, and only later did it serve as a shop for dispensing ironmongery, builders' commodities, paint etc. From the early 1960s through to the 80s, it made an ideal venue for Anvil

Antiques – in fact many visitors were often more interested in the building than the stock! It has now reverted to residential use.

Our buildings in Station Road are all listed, and the blacksmith shop is unusual in this area for its construction in brick and flint. The traverse is now incorporated as part of the workshop, but much of the original building can still be seen and many features, albeit by luck and chance, still remain.

It is worthy of note that Melton had three blacksmith shops at one time: in the Street, Station Road, and near Wilford Bridge. The last one, Wilford Place, with its quay, public house, and cottages, was a hamlet away from the main village. In addition Page and Girling's foundry had their own blacksmith shop (still virtually intact, and hidden away behind 20th century buildings).

Jack was very proud of being one of the last genuine all-purpose blacksmiths in the area. The range of work which we have carried out over the years would certainly seem to justify this claim. A reflection of his personality was how the blacksmith shop came over the years to be a meeting place for many 'old stagers', who habitually could be found there putting village and world affairs to rights. It is a credit to my father that despite his lack of business acumen, the business steadily expanded, as did the range of services offered; at the time of his death we employed four men and we look to modest growth in the years ahead.

*Robert Blake*
*Blake's Agricultural*
*Engineers*
*(Melton) Ltd*

**Bilby's business card, late 19th century**

## *Jack Blake*

**Jack Blake, 1989**

Jack was a true 'character', never lost for words and whose motto was "never give up". He was a man of many talents but had no real interest in money. He was fond of saying: "I will get you going", and this he did, many times for many people, and for well over his allotted 'three score years and ten'.

Right from an early age, Jack had always been a practical worker and when at school, which he didn't start until he was ten years old, would climb out of his bedroom window, slide down the plum tree and work in the shed, making egg-cups, linen pegs and spinning-tops, often not returning to bed until three in the morning.

Nothing was too much trouble for him to sort out. In fact he loved a challenge. When cooking ranges were first introduced there seemed to be a problem in heating the ovens but Jack soon found that it was all a question of draught and having too much cold air. He often used to say: "Paper talk is no good, it's common sense which you need. I have learned more by watching others and keeping it in my head."

Jack came to love Suffolk and was well-known to local farmers when he visited their farms with his threshing engines. Sometimes, especially as old age increasingly took its toll, he would not be feeling very well, but never gave up; he was never one to let anybody down. He continued to be 'on duty' until he was over ninety, advising and giving practical help at the Melton forge.

*Peggy Cole*
*1, Park Lane*
*Charsfield (Akenfield)*
*Woodbridge*

# Bob Daines remembers...

I was born in 1907 in the Parish of Melton. My earliest recollection is of my 19 year old sister coming home and telling us she had been to the Market Hill, Woodbridge to hear the first World War declared. Within a month she had died of pneumonia. Medical science has done a lot to prevent such tragedies these days. I lived opposite what is now Melton Playing Field, known then as the Park. The Welsh Horse were about the first to occupy the Park which within weeks of the outbreak became a hutted camp. The very large number of horses on parade in the road as we went to school caused great excitement to us children. The Norfolk Regiment and the Buffs also occupied the Park. Frequently drafts for France were played to Melton Station by band and we boys used to run alongside. The sight of some of these mature family men crying on the way to the Station will remain with me till I die. For at times during the Great War it seemed that they were going to almost certain death. My family

**Church gates, by Page & Girling**

**Cast iron gate pillars, made by Page & Girling, c1880**

has read the East Anglian Daily Times as long as I can remember but I hope my descendants will never see page after page of casualties as was the case then.

I was educated at the old elementary school and we wrote on slates. As a reward for arithmetic and spelling we sometimes won a slate pencil but we had no slate at home.

Christmas to us children was a wonderful time. We were a large family but everyone was at home for Christmas and I am sure we were just as happy with a shilling for a present as children are today with a new bicycle.

Whilst at school Tilling Stevens started the open topped bus service. The fare to Woodbridge was one Imperial penny. Inflation has increased this to over 70 times as much and I honestly believe there are more people walk to Woodbridge now than there were then. Progress?

At St. Andrew's Church, Melton, we had a very large all male choir. The choir stalls were not sufficient to accommodate the choir and several chairs had to be used. We were a paid choir. We received 3/6d. (17.5p) per quarter. Some boys attended Matins and Evensong regularly in order to qualify. The choir had an annual outing to Felixstowe either by chain ferry at Bawdsey or via Martlesham when we had to walk up Brightwell Hill to allow the horse-drawn waggonette to negotiate.

Whilst at school we had lots of fun at the Annual Sutton Lamb Sale held on the Church Meadow, now St. Andrew's Place. Huge flocks of sheep were driven along the roads. There was no transport other than the trains and they had to walk miles from country districts. We had great fun trying to catch sheep, rugby fashion, that had broken away from the flock.

As we became a little older we boys played all sorts of pranks in the village but the village policeman was a law unto himself. Many a time he would stop a lad and tan his backside with a cane he carried down the leg of his trousers. If the boy shouted: "I haven't done anything" the constable would say: "Never mind. I will get the right one next time." Generally parents were on the side of the constable and if the boy complained to his father he would get another clip round the ear.

Many Melton men worked at Page and Girling's foundry and the bell summoning the men to work could be heard a long way off. Quite a number of men were employed by Bilby Bros., Builders, opposite Melton Church, and present day workers will smile when they read that one of the brothers used to stand at the gate with his watch in his hand checking in the men.

The River Deben at Melton often had five or six barges unloading stone for the roads at Melton Quay near Wilford Bridge, and corn and coal at Melton Dock. It was fascinating watching men carry 16 stones of corn across a long plank that went up and down a couple of feet with every step. One false step and they would have been in the water. The only time these men were unskilled was on pay day!

I will try to record a number of changes that have taken place during my lifetime in the village that is very dear to me. I have never wanted to live anywhere else. I will try to describe Melton from the Woodbridge end as I knew it in my youth. Before Messrs. Teddy

Early 1900s advert for Page & Girling, Agricultural & Horticultural Engineers

**Teddy Fairhead and Jack Sawyer**

Fairhead and Jack Sawyer started their business with an ex-Army hut, the site was a small meadow on which was a tiny hut where people could purchase paraffin. I remember we could buy fireworks there.

The house that was built for Mr. Tile at the rear of Fairhead and Sawyers was the site of the original Woodbridge Steam Laundry, proprietor H.P. Kirk, for many years a Parish Councillor. The meadow where Mr. J. Smith lives next to Blyth Hasel was the Sheep Hurdle Makers Yard, a thriving business at the time. Before being developed the meadow between River Cottage and the Hurdle Makers was known as Speargrass Meadow, the home of Melton Cricket and Tennis Clubs. One of the Cricket Club's regular fixtures was at Sudbourne Hall. The Lyon family lived at the Hall. Mr. D. Lyon played for Somerset and B.H. Lyon for Gloucestershire. I was thrilled one Saturday when as a teenager I was called upon to play and in the Sudbourne team was Mr. D. Lyon, one of the outstanding batsmen in England at the time.

It may be interesting to recall that John Crane of the bakery, now converted to private quarters at the Post Office, used to deliver an urn of tea and trays of cakes (by horse and cart) to the cricket match at one shilling per head.

I started work at the Bakery on leaving school but did not stay long. I went to learn my father's trade at the Basket Works down Daines Lane, where I was born. I stayed with my father until I was 27. With tractors taking the place of horses on the farms and plastics becoming increasingly used the basket trade became very hard to get a living by and I left the business. Recently, after about 40 years, I had the opportunity of trying my hand again and it gave me great satisfaction that I had not lost the know-how.

From Daines Lane to the Old Water Works, the footpath was a direct line. Nowadays one has a job to follow it because of development. There was a very popular bathing place at Hackney opposite Fayrefield Road. During the great floods of 1939 the river wall on the Sutton side was broken and never repaired. Prior to this on the Melton side there was a lovely stretch of hard beach and it seemed in summer that half the women in the village went there to picnic after collecting their children from school. After the breach in the wall the hard beach quickly became as muddy as the rest of the river. Hackney was so popular at one time that a school master at Melton formed a water polo club.

The whole of the present school playing field was a mass of roses in summer – Morse's Nursery.

At the White House (Melton House) where the traffic lights are, lived a Mr. Brasnett who kept a lot of pigs. During the First World War we gathered acorns which would be bought from us. I have never heard of acorns being collected for pigs since. Later in the early 1920s I remember the excitement when we learned that a well known Dutch artist* and his wife were coming to live at Melton House. The village soon accepted the sight of its own resident artist sketching and painting in the area. For the honoured few there was the opportunity to sit for one's portrait to be painted; Van Someren's real forte was as a portrait painter and examples of his work are still to be found in the village today.

When I was at school, soldiers were billeted in the old gaol. I remember during the winter snows we boys used to roll dead mice (of which there was a plentiful supply at that time) into snowballs and throw them into the soldiers' quarters. Of course if we were caught we paid for it.

Opposite the Melton Corn and Coal Office is still the Round House (the Bowery) which was Miss Ross' sweet shop - very popular with school children. Her takings could not have been very large as I feel sure most of her customers had just one halfpenny to spend.

In Woods Lane, opposite Mr. Wells' house, was Hall Farm,

* Major Edward Van Someren was of Dutch origin

with ploughed land this side and a meadow the other. At one time I used to collect a can of milk there after school and walk with it to Bury Hill, five times a week for a shilling per week.

I remember the lamp lighter coming along Melton Road where the gas lamp standards stood in the gutter. Telegraph poles also stood in the gutter and although motor traffic was few and far between there were several accidents, partly due I suppose to the position of these posts and partly to the inefficient steering and brakes on vehicles at that time. And of course according to the law if one could drive a flock of sheep one could drive a car. There were no driving tests until much later.

Coming into the street quite a feature of our village was opposite the Chapel where everything the farmer required for his horses was to be found. William Booth the village blacksmith (also landlord of the Horse and Groom), Jim Beedon the wheelwright and Tom Spink the harness maker, all side by side. Round the blacksmith's forecourt were iron railings and I must tell a story that was just before my time. My uncle told me that an old gentleman* used to drive a donkey cart to Melton Chapel from Bredfield and whilst in Chapel the lads used to put the donkey in the shafts in reverse, much to the annoyance of the old man.

For many years I played football on the Church Meadow where the Lamb Sale was. The top goalposts were just about where Mrs. Birdseye's bungalow now stands (1, St Andrews Close).

**Daines the basketmaker**

Opposite Church Meadow was Church Farm from where our local milkman used to operate with his handcart – Mr. Pratt.

Most of my leisure time during my life has been given to sport. I helped to found the Old Melton St. Andrew's Football Club with Mr. Bentham as Chairman, and the Cricket Club after World War Two, and I have been a life member of these Clubs as well as the Bowls Club. I have perhaps given too much of my time to sport but I have the satisfaction of knowing it has helped to give pleasure to hundreds of young men. Some unfortunately did not survive World War Two.

*Bob Daines*
*1907-1992*

**Stripping the willow for Daines the basketmaker**

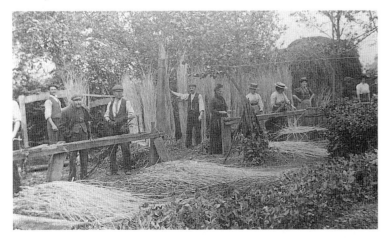

* This gentleman is likely to feature in a forthcoming book by Robert Blake

21  Early 20th century photograph showing the Old Church from Decoy Farm.
N.B. Train in background getting-up-steam for the long incline from Melton Station to Campsea Ashe

# Religious life

## The Rector, Mark Sanders, writes

The list of rectors goes back to the early middle ages, and may go back further still, perhaps to Queen, and later Saint, Etheldreda, of whose dowry land Melton was part; her name is still present in its shortened form, St Audry, and in the fact that the Old Church was dedicated to St Andrew with St Etheldreda. This great Christian lady founded the abbey - now Cathedral of Ely - and it seems unlikely that she would have totally neglected the religious needs of Meltonians in the mid-seventh century. In those days the role of the priest would have been to establish the Christian religion in the first place, as this had been a great area for paganism, as the Sutton Hoo ship burial shows.

The link with Ely has remained through the ages, and the Dean and Chapter - the clergy who run the Cathedral at Ely - have the right to appoint clergy to this parish. So back in 1987 when I was looking at the possibility of coming to minister here, Clare and I had a thorough interview with them, a good lunch and the promise of the tour of the cathedral - sadly that was not forthcoming as it would have saved us the entrance fee!

Over the generations has the job of Rector changed? Probably. In the Middle Ages and after, the clergy gained their income from tithes and from land they farmed for themselves, called glebe. Now the glebe and tithes have gone but the pastoral work has increased considerably as the parish has grown in population. Most of the acreage is now under houses rather than crops.

But in some important respects the job is still the same: to help the people of Melton praise and worship God through the Word of Scripture and the sacraments. Offering services is the single most important expectation, and it is a great privilege as it often involves one at a very deep level in the lives of others.

Especially in the Victorian period rectors stayed a long time, the Rev. G.C. Watson being Rector for fifty plus years. Not only must he have seen generations of the same family "hatched, matched and despatched"; he also had the energy at the end of his ministry to realise the need for a new church in the heart of the village and over £3,000 was raised to build it. Inevitably sometimes the worship and the place in which it is done tend to loom large. Once up, buildings take a huge labour of love to keep them in good repair. Encouraging the village to take this on has been the task of Rectors and churchwardens through the generations. Sadly it can seem to take over, but the attempt, through festivals, has been to make fund raising positive and fun.

It has been our aim to bring the different parts of Melton together through the celebrations. The parish is a funny shape, and its segmented communities can look in different directions. The church should be a focus of unity for the village, providing events and worship for those who wish to join in, whatever their level of commitment. In times of need we (both clergy and laity) offer support and empathy which is on-going; this is, and must be, at the heart of the Christian community. The values and beliefs of the church help to shape an understanding of sharing and worth within a community. I hope the fact that we draw people from all corners of the parish and beyond suggests that some of this has been successful.

So what does a rector do? A difficult question to answer as one day can be totally different from the next. Most days include a chunk of visiting, some worship and prayers, meetings of church or other organisations, routine administration. Prayers are offered for those who are sick or in need, services thought about and prepared. Time is meant to be spent reading but that often gets squeezed out. Altogether it adds up to a week of 60+ hours quite regularly with the day starting at 7.10 with prayers and often going on until after 9 p.m. It can be a tiring, if rich, combination.

At the heart of the job is working with others to try and express something of God's love for other people, and to help others express a prayer or praise of God. The privilege in this is immense.

*A Personal Postscript*

When Clare and I first came we lived in what we were told was "Upper Melton", in what had been lovely woods, which tragically are even more under threat now. Living up there, commuting the 1.4 miles to the church, Melton really felt like a suburb of Woodbridge. If it wasn't for the church and my job with it we might have been excused for thinking we lived there rather than in Melton. As I went up and down Woods Lane, sometimes as many as three times a day, I began to wonder with the position of the village sign whether I did live in Melton or not!

Living down by the church gives a different perspective. The old part of the village is more obvious. Even though most of the houses do not seem that old there is a greater sense of identity. Happily the traffic lights no longer seem the centre of the village

Having lived in both areas it seems there is no one answer to whether Melton is still a village or has become a suburb. There are many who live within the church parish boundaries who worship in Woodbridge and look to our larger neighbour for everything. There are some who live there but come to Melton because they like the feel of the village. Perhaps Melton defies any one single description.

As a resident I give thanks for many of the good things which we share. The beautiful area which surrounds us, and that there is green space to walk the dog within easy reach of wherever I'm visiting. The mixture of people and housing means a variety of outlook and interest. Being a 'suburb' of Woodbridge means having the resources of that lovely market town and Ipswich close by. I was not surprised to discover that Melton is one of the most sought after areas for housing within Suffolk Coastal – it shows a lot of sense.

*Rev. Mark Sanders*
*Melton Rectory*

**Rev. Mark Sanders and his wife, Clare, on her ordination in 1994**

Kind permission of The East Anglian Daily Times

# The Church in Melton

The present Parish church, St. Andrew's, was consecrated in May 1868, at a ceremony which filled the new building to its limit. A new church had been needed for a long time - the old one being so far from the centre of the village that it had become a trek on Sundays for the majority of the congregation. The Dissenters had built a chapel in the Street and no doubt the diocese felt that they were in danger of losing members.

The Bishop of Norwich, the Rt. Rev. John Pelham, in whose diocese Melton then was, gave the opening address. He was an old fashioned Evangelical and his fine dissertation on the work of the parish priest is relevant today, and worth quoting in part:

*"When the word of God is faithfully and lovingly preached, when the ordinances of the Church are devoutly and intelligently minis t e r e d by a pastor whose personal and domestic ministrations in the parish supplement his ministrations in the Church, the truth commends itself more forcibly to the consciences, and the minister gains the respect and affection of the people committed to his charge, and the objects for which the ministry was ordained and for which the Church was built are then realised and appreciated and willing hearts with even weakened hands and straitened means will do more, and do it better, than cold hearts with the largest means will ever dream of."*

As the church had cost the modest sum of £4349 (currently insured for £1.6 million, which is well over 300 times the original building cost) it is evident that straitened means had been a factor in the case of St. Andrew's, but the Bishop's remarks about the duties of the pastor sum up the work of the church throughout its history, and continue to apply today. This is recognised in the activities of the parish, which, although they have become rather more diverse and complicated than in Bishop Pelham's time, are still, essentially, a merging of spiritual guidance with everyday preoccupation and have recently been set out by the present Rector in his "A Look into 1994". There, church activities are listed under 9 headings:

St. Andrews new church, 1868 *

1 Worship and Music - the choirs of the two morning services, readers and intercessors, service preparation.
2 Family - preparation for Baptism and follow up, marriage, Small Fry (parents and infants), family matters
3 Youth Ministry - Fish Club (Sunday School), Chips (7-11 years old), In-B-Teens (11-14 years old), Duke of Edinburgh Group (14+years old) affiliated to the national scheme, Confirmation, special events and social gatherings.
4 Adult ministry - Study groups, Open Door (Ladies' Group), programmes of studies, social functions.
5 Pastoral care - Good Neighbours (help in the neighbourhood, visiting etc.), bereavement care, friendliness to newcomers, crisis care.
6 Church and village - Mission events, involvement in village organisations and social responsibility.
7 Larger Involvement - role in deanery and diocese, other churches, Charities, and the world.
8 Buildings and Land - Church, churchyards, church room, restoration and repairs, fund raising.
9 Communications and Finance - covenanting and giving, budgeting, typing and printing, parish magazine.

* NB Page & Girling's fine cast-iron gates were installed in the early 1870s

During the recent 125th anniversary events, the linking of the church to parish life was emphasised, with a series of group meetings entitled "Connections". Some of the activities might puzzle Bishop Pelham if he heard of them today and he would find it helpful to pick up a leaflet from the Rectory describing some of them in greater detail. It would take more time to explain to him why there are two prayer books in use in the same church, but essentially the work is the same work that he promoted, and he would have endorsed the Pastoral letter from the House of Bishops, particularly the commitment by the Church of England to serve all the nation, and

*"the proclamation of the Gospel in worship, word, sacrament and service; pastoral ministry; access to public worship; and witness to Christian truth at every level of public life."*

**Melton Choir, 1948: Rev. R. Hurd centre; Verger, Mr George Wright, top left; Churchwarden, Mr Fred Bloss, middle right**

It is unlikely that in 1868 St. Andrew's offered such a large range of services as the Church offers today. Every Sunday churchgoers have an 8.00 Communion service, a family service at 9.30 and a Matins at 11.15 using the Book of Common Prayer. Also, there is a Communion service on Wednesdays at 10.00 a.m. and an Evensong at 3.30 p.m.

Melton is an active and surprisingly centred parish – surprisingly because a look at the map would suggest that as a village it is an appendage to Woodbridge, with the parish boundary running down the middle of streets in places. In spite of this it is decidedly conscious of itself as a separate place, and much of this awareness is because of St. Andrew's. With the numbers on the electoral roll as a guide, it is among the top 5% for attendance in the diocese, and this is reflected in the strong support that it is given in its fund raising and for all its various activities.

*C. A. Latimer*
*P.C.C. Secretary*
*3 The Street, Melton*

**Interior of St. Andrews before the screen was donated, c1935**

**Exterior and interior photographs of the Old Church and a 19th century watercolour by Laura Churchyard**

Churchyard watercolours

Edward van Someren watercolours of "Bloss's Barn", Hall Farm Road

# From the 'Suffolk Pulpit' 1857-61

"In Church only 50 worshippers, some came in carriages, a few with servants in attendance upon them. Not a dozen of the working class present. With a small gallery for singers, we saw no schools, no free benches filled with aged people, none of the industrious poor... we saw in fact nothing to indicate that the efforts made by the Church and her representative within the locality were at all appreciated by any of those classes for whose benefit the State Church is sometimes said to be working. The Rev. G. C. Watson is not, we believe, resident in the place... he is assisted by a Curate in a very dull and spiritless style. Mr. Watson, about sixty years of age, is of florid healthy looks. We could discern no evidence either that the works in which the Rev. gentleman was engaged were congenial to him or that he had any special fitness for it... His defects and weaknesses enhanced by a genteel laissez-faire manner.

We thought in justice to state that the weather was exceedingly unfavourable and the Church at Melton is placed at a most unconscionable distance from the village. The removal of the Church... would bring such instruction as the Established Church affords within the reach of the aged, the infirm and the sick, besides rendering Church-going far from possible, not to say comfortable even to the robust during the winter season."

(The Church was removed – i.e. a new church provided in the village proper – seven or eight years later, and the old Church became as it still is – a haunt for mourners and brass rubbers.)

**15th century Font depicting the Seven Sacraments, one of only 38 surviving examples in England (now in the new Church)**

**Rare triple brass in Melton Old Church**

**Thomas Churchyard's painting of the Old Church**

## Melton Old Church - A Village Peculiar*

The Saxon Manor of Melton belonged to the Abbot of Ely, and in the opinion of the historian, Mr. Norman Scarfe, a Church has stood on the site from that time. A Saxon Amulet was found in the churchyard in the 19th century.

The first recorded Rector was William, son of Theodwine, in 1146. There is a rare triple Brass in the Nave, which depicts a Priest in academic dress with his parents, dated C. 1436.

When, in 1977, the Old Church was made redundant, it was not fully understood that this could mean disposal for other purposes, so that in 1979, when a proposal was approved for conversion to an Anglo/Norwegian Study Centre, Melton people felt affronted, for many generations of local people had worshipped there and lay buried in the old churchyard. The Church was considered an essential part of village heritage. Therefore a society was formed in 1980 to find an alternative use. Meetings were held, funds raised, and the Church Commissioners agreed to a new Redundancy Scheme.

It was largely at the instigation and under the leadership of the late Mr Peter Hope of Red Towers that the plan to save the Church was launched. Peter admirably carried on his family's commitment to all aspects of Melton life. He was Chairman of the Parish Council for over 30 years and a lifelong worshipper at St Andrew's Church, having been baptised there. He was a man of many parts; few knew much of his philanthropic work and his many acts of kindness to Meltonians over the years.

In 1982, the Old Church passed into the care of the Melton Old Church Society, a Registered Charity, to be used for Christian, Community and Educational purposes. A Trust Fund was formed which will provide for the future care and maintenance of the building.

In 1983 the Society undertook the costly work of re-tiling the roof and renewing the guttering. During the work, rare 14th century glazed ridge tiles came to light.

In November 1984 it was decided that a programme of work still to be done should be drawn up. The cost of this was estimated at £20,000. The Historic Buildings Council was approached for a 50% grant, which was kindly agreed, provided that the Society raised a similar sum over the next three years .

The work undertaken was the refacing of the Tower, the renewal of stonework where necessary, and the re-leading of the windows.

By the end of 1986 the restoration was completed and the Committee felt the Church was in good condition to last many years.

However, because Events such as Concerts and Lectures are held where refreshments are served, the new Fire Safety Regulations which came into being in 1989 required that a second exit to the Church be made with appropriate lighting. This entailed a lot of work on design, planning permission, etc. An opening was already in place behind the Altar, which had previously led to a small Vestry. A suitable oak door was chosen and fitted. In the same year, deathwatch beetle had been found in the roof and this had to be treated at a cost of £1,048 plus VAT. This together with the provision of the oak door was a considerable drain on the funds.

As well as Concerts and Lectures, Picture and Craft Exhibitions are held; also the traditional Service of Evensong on All Souls' Day. The Society has over two hundred members.

The Church is available for other Societies to use, with the permission of the Committee.

The Society is greatly indebted to all who have supported and encouraged the work of this project since its inception and who have helped to ensure that the Church does not become a burden to the Parish.

*Mrs. G.M. Blake*
*Chairman*

* A Peculiar – a church not under the jurisdiction of the diocesan bishop

# Removal of the Methodist Chapel, 1861

"A mechanical operation of considerable interest took place at Melton near Woodbridge when the Primitive Methodist Chapel was removed in a mass 15 feet from its original foundation. The removal was rendered necessary by a verdict of a jury, who, as it originally stood, pronounced it a nuisance* to a gentleman's house** standing on adjoining ground. The Chapel, a neat and unpretentious structure, is of red and white bricks built 1860. Its size is 33 feet 6 inches long by 31 feet 6 inches wide, and the height to the eaves 17 feet. A schoolroom and vestry adjoined the Chapel, but these have been pulled down to afford greater facility for the removal, and are to be rebuilt.

The removal was accomplished as follows: the base course around the Chapel was entirely cut away, and beams 13 x 7 were inserted longitudinally, and firmly wedged to the underside of the walls with fir needles, whilst support was further gained by transverse beams placed at intervals. The former beams rested immediately upon seven fir slips 12 inches by 7 inches which formed the way upon which the structure was to travel, and which were laid to a rise of 1 in 180 so that the building had not only to be removed in a horizontal direction but uphill also. The walls were firmly bolted together with two sets of $1^{1}/4''$ bar iron running round the outside of the building, and one $1^{1}/2''$ bolt through the chapel from side to side. The removal was effected by the application of two screw faces to one side of the building (pushing it forward) and three pairs of double screws to the other side (pulling it), the ways or beams on which the building travelled being well greased to prevent friction, and to ensure greater ease in transit. The Pastor sat in his pulpit throughout the whole operation with a glass of water beside him; the movement of the building

was so smooth that neither the Pastor nor the glass of water were upset! In three hours after commencing, the Chapel was safely lodged on its new foundation and presenting not even a scratch or the appearance of a crack; a good deal of credit is due to Messrs. Collins, Millwrights*, for the easy and successful apparatus by which the building was removed."

*From a contemporary report*

* The Collins brothers were highly skilled millwrights, also with a reputation as versatile machinists. It was in this capacity that Thomas Collins undertook to move the chapel the crucial fifteen feet.

**The photograph shows the Chapel's removal in progress. The 'protective barrier' (left) was erected to obstruct non-paying spectators witnessing the event. The 'emerged' White House can be seen in the background**

* ancient lights    ** The White House

# Perambulation of the Village, 1815

"From Wilford Bridge, leaving the lost Marsh on the left side, a mile on, at an Elm tree in Dr. Syers' meadow called Needle Meadow, shortly to cross the river through a hole in the River called Needle Meadow Hole. Proceed along the side of Mr. Jenney's Mill Meadow bypassing a marked Oak and Dole Posts to Ballot's Hole in the river, where Mr. Brightwell stripped and swam across to an old style, and continued to Ufford Street, and took in the hamlet nearly opposite the Lion Inn and back to Ballot's Hole. Keep to the ditch on the right. Go over a steep hedge by a ladder and into the road. Cross the road into an Arched Gateway in Mr. Edwards' Wall. Leave house and garden on right and proceed to the Barn at a marked Elm and cross to Mr. Brooke's Orchard and then straight across the field to Mr. Brooke's Plantation in N.W. direction. Leave the Plantation in Ufford on your Right, pass a marked Oak and Pollarded Ash to the Turnpike. Cross into Hackeries Lane, At left hand corner is a cross filled up with stones. At another marked Oak leading to a Gateway, leaving the House of Industry on your left proceed through Mr. Whincopp's fields to another Gateway, leading to Mr. Brooke's farm House. Turn Right into Cross Pightle and proceed across the field called Nine Acre field to Mr. Whincopp's Gate leading to his Farm. Go through the centre of the two cart sheds into the road leading to the Farm House, pass through the middle of the pigstyes to the pump and go on through the Backhouse. Go through the Window and on to the road, and leave the Farm House in Bredfield, and come to the cottages, where formerly stood a Malt House, into Mr. Whincopp's Great Gates, where is a cross filled with stones. Cross the field to a very old Dole Post marked B.P., proceed along the hedge to a gate and on to Mr. Jenney's Farm House, where you turn left to where the Old Road was opposite Mr. Jenney's House until you come opposite the Canal in the garden. Go through an Avenue of trees and the centre of the Canal to the garden pales. Turn left at the corner. Go in a straight line to a marked Oak in the fence near the Nursery. Proceed to another Pollarded Oak, go round the side of the Nursery to a Pond, then turn left along the path by a large Scotch Fir, cross a quickset hedge and into Coach Field. Continue to the Pond in the middle of this field and on to Mr. Abraham Brook's field in a straight line to a marked Oak nearby a style and lane where two gateposts are marked, also a cross filled with stones. Go up this road till Hoe Lane. Turn left at the corner of Mr. Newson's Meadow. Cross this field and hedge and go on to the Road at the Corner opposite the Barn to another cross filled with stones. Leave the Barn on your left, turn down the road on the left, leaving the Wind Mills on the right and Mr. Pytches' house on the left. Continue to the Yarmouth Turnpike Road. Cross it, and go into Mr. Lankester's garden. Leave his new house on your left in the Parish of Melton, and continue in a straight line over the Delf onto the Wall to a small oak near the Barrs on the Wall nearby opposite Little Hoe Farm in Sutton. Turn left onto the Wall and continue till you come to Wilford Bridge from whence you first started."

*From a contemporary record*

*The Perambulation, or 'Beating the Bounds', was undertaken by the Rector (1815 Rev. Christopher Watson M.A.) accompanied by the inhabitants of Melton and took place regularly on Rogation Sunday.*

Twentieth century key to the Perambulation:

From Wilford Bridge northwards to Melton Mill (from the Mill the present differs as to how much of the meadow land around the Lion Inn is part of Ufford).
Mr Brook and his family lived for many years at Ufford Place.
The Barn is Block's Barn and Turnpike is Yarmouth Road.
The House of Industry became St. Audry's.
Mr Whincroft lived at Foxborrow Hall – the Parish Boundary passed through and between the Farm house and the Backhouse!
The Canal was in the garden of Bredfield House.
Hoe Lane is now Haugh Lane.
The Barn stood on the corner of Bredfield Road (next to Brownings) Northfield Corner and Pytches Road.
The Windmills stood on Victoria Road.
Mr Pytches' house and Mount Pleasant are now Melton Grange.
Little Hoe is now Little Hoo.

31    The 18th century central block of the former House of Industry

# St Audry's

*Suffolk Lunatic Asylum*

"Suffolk Lunatic Asylum which stands in a healthy and airy situation, near Woodbridge, but in Melton Parish, was originally erected as a House of Industry for the parishes of Loes and Wilford Hundreds, which were incorporated for the maintenance of their poor in 1765, but disincorporated in 1827 when the building was purchased by the county magistrates, chiefly for the reception of pauper lunatics. Whilst a workhouse, it had at times 250 inmates, and there are now within its walls some 450 patients, labouring under the worst of human maladies, insanity. They are all Suffolk paupers, for Whom their respective parishes pay at the rate of 10s. 6d. per week per head. This useful and well-regulated establishment, including the purchase of the grounds and the original buildings, and the subsequent alterations, enlargements and improvements, with the furniture had cost about £37,000 in 1844, and the asylum was considerably enlarged and improved in 1850, at a further outlay of £2,000. Though it is not so imposing in external appearance as some other county asylums its internal arrangements and domestic economy are of the highest order. It was one of the first asylums in which the non-restraint system in treatment of insanity was introduced; indeed its skilful and humane superintendent (Dr. Kirkman) has never resorted to personal restraint for more than forty years; he relies upon kindness and giving practical employment to patients. Recreation is provided by work on the farm, gardens and pleasure grounds. The Government Commissioners inspect the premises yearly, and a committee of visiting county magistrates meets here every alternate Friday. The total number of patients admitted since the opening of the asylum in 1827 to July 1874 was 4,299 – the annual charge per patient in 1873 being £27. 6s. 0d."

*Taken from White's Suffolk Directory, 1874.*

**Steam engine working at the hospital laundry**

# The relationship to the Village

The relationship between St. Audry's Hospital and Melton village was always complex and somewhat ambiguous. For generations 'Melton' for ordinary people in the area was identified with the hospital, while much misunderstanding towards mental illness and the aims of those responsible for patients' care prevailed. White's Authoritative County Directory of 1874 labels all those patients in the then named 'Suffolk Lunatic Asylum' as simply suffering from insanity. However from the outset both asylum/hospital and village benefited from their close proximity. Firstly secure employment was available for many parishioners.

From the early years of its establishment as an asylum limited staff accommodation was on offer. Redwald House, the Chief Medical Superintendent's residence, Tom Cooper's Lodge (situated at the back entrance), East Lodge for the Chief Male Nurse, South Lodge the Chief Engineer's, and the farm bailiff lived at Grove Farm House (until the farm as a whole was sold in the 1950s); unmarried female nurses from the 1930s at the Nurses' Home. (Previously only a few unmarried male nurses lived "on-the-wards".) The 16 houses – Upper Melton Terrace – constructed in the early 1900s were supplemented by a further 8 dwellings, South Close, some 60 years later. These offered good accommodation much above the standards of the area and until the ideal of home ownership firmly took root in the early Thatcher years represented an additional incentive for employment at St Audry's.

Staff living out would travel to work, so, as St. Audry's expanded (see Appendix 5 ) its importance for local employment increased. Opportunities to improve oneself through internal promotion and, from the mid-19th century, obtain a sense of vocation were of salient importance for attracting and retaining staff. These factors, together with the 1909 Asylum Officers' Superannuation Act, offered a good pension scheme and help to explain why many families worked for generations in St. Audry's. Notable must be the case of the Smith family, who achieved a total of well over 200 years' combined service. This dates back to 1872 when George Smith became a charge nurse; three of his

**1972:**
**Iain, Audrey and Arthur Smith, whose family worked at the hospital for a total of over 240 years**

sons, Frank, Arthur and Albert, worked at St. Audry's, as did his grandson Arthur and great grandson Iain. In fact, George Smith became Melton's first Asylum officer to receive the pension, in 1910, a year after the 1909 Act was passed. Other families also can trace service through many generations, but as one such recently told me, "We never divulged to outsiders where we worked. We were like Income Tax Officers. We happily talked about living in Melton but avoided or, worse, 'froze' when uncomplimentary remarks were made about St. Audry's."

St Audry's had expanded from the 1870s onwards and within ten years, by 1885 the patients and the staff employed for their care outnumbered the inhabitants of Melton village.

Many local businesses profited from supplying the needs of the hospital, especially before the days of centralised buying. However, the stigma of having members of one's family either as patients or working for St. Audry's continued until after the Second World War.

**Early 20th century
photograph of St Audry's**

Changes in the care and general perceived needs of the mentally ill have developed radically over the last 20 years. The ideal of community care has made a large institutional establishment such as St. Audry's an anachronism, so its eventual closure had been anticipated long before 1993. Much had been achieved by the 'open policy' introduced from the 1960s, when restrictions on patients were steadily lessened. Open days where the public were invited to visit and see the workings of the hospital and to meet patients helped in this respect. However, for some staff there was a strong feeling of betrayal as policies developed and they questioned whether all patients could be given true 'asylum' within the community. Sadly after more than 200 years' service to the community St. Audry's now stands emptied and shuttered, awaiting an uncertain future.

## History of St Audry's

*Phase 1:*

*1765*
An Act of Parliament decreed that provision be made for the better Relief and employment of the Poor in the Hundreds of Looes and Wilford. (Hundreds were medieval divisions of Counties). Meeting called at Wickham Market White Hart to elect a Corporation to carry out the term of the Act.

*1767*
Melton House opened. Managed by 15 Members of the Corporation who met each Monday. Day to day administration carried out by a Governor Steward or Matron and a Clergyman. Prime function House of Industry. Materials purchased included Flax, wood, hemp, cotton thread, iron, stone, wood and leather and according to the 1765 Act "Profits" from the work to be distributed to the industrious and skilful in proportion to the quality and perfection of their work. Also the Governor and Matron took 2d in the £1 from the profits.

*(1801: 501 Melton pop.)*

*1826*
Another Act repealed the original Act and appointed trustees to wind up the estate and purchase the premises, land and fixtures. The purchase was completed for £10,000. All inmates were returned to villages and hamlets. The land comprised 30 acres at the time.

*1827*
Building bought by County Authority Reconstructed to house 130 patients.

**Dr Whitwell (medical supervisor 1896 - 1924) in driving seat**

*Phase 2:*

*1829*
Between 1826-9 the buildings were converted and extended to provide an Asylum for 130 patients and renamed Suffolk County Asylum. The Asylum was managed by a Committee of Visiting Justices. There were 18 officers and staff. During the next few decades £30,000 was spent on new buildings. Dr. Wallett first Medical Superintendent.

*1832*
Dr. Wallett left. Dr. J. Kirkman commences.

*(1841: 217 patients. 980 Melton pop.)*

*1844*
Addition to male & female Wards + 120 patients. (Block 2 & 3)

*1846*
Farming operations stepped up by purchase of more land.

*(1846: 24 acres: 1900: 233 acres)*

*(1855: 269 patients. 1069 Melton pop.)*

**Construction of water tower, 1886**

*1856*
Dormitories (later housed St Audry's Museum).

*1862/64*
More additions.

*1874*
450 patients and approx. 50 staff. Working as sportsmen, musicians, tradesmen and keepers.

*1876*
Dr. Kirkman retired. Dr. W. Eager commences.

*1885-87*
Additions included male Wards 7, 8, 9; kitchen enlarged; new recreation hall; new water tower and laundry.

*1890*
The Lunacy Act brought reforms in the method of committing patients to Lunatic Asylums by empowering Justices of the Peace to certify people. Numbers increased rapidly and by 1904 more Ward blocks, a new laundry boiler house, waterworks, church and other buildings.

*1892*
Melton Water Works built after new water bore sunk at Station Road. (Demolished 1989 after sale for private housing development.)

*1893*
More Wards added male & female 10 & 11. Accommodation now 620.

*1896*
Dr. Eager retired. Dr. J.R. Whitwell appointed.

*1902*
Now 900 beds available and 224 staff in post. male & female 10, 11, 12, 13, 14 added plus Isolation Hospital (Whitwell House; Bakehouse; Mortuary; Medical Supt. house; farm buildings; Boiler house; Butchers shop; East & South Lodges; 16 houses (Upper Melton Terrace); electric light replaces gas.

*Phase 3:*

*1907*
The Asylum renamed Suffolk District Asylum with St. Clements serving the Borough of Ipswich.

*(1911:· 817 patients. 2058 Melton pop.)*

*1913/14*
Cottages built (Melton Terrace).

*(1922: 900 patients. 2214 Melton pop.)*

*1924 (1916?)*
St. Audry's Hospital now appears on Annual Reports.
Dr. Whitwell retires:  Dr. Brooks-Keith commences.

*1927*
Nurses home opened 19.5.1927.

*1930*
Mental Treatment Act made it possible for patients to be admitted of their own free will, recognising the need for treatment at an earlier stage.

*1934*
Occupational Therapy started on Male 3 for male patients only.

*1935*
1250 patients now in residence. 700 female 550 male.

*1947*
Occupational Therapy introduced for female patients on female Ward 201/2. Even before the introduction of O/T patients were always employed in laundry, farm and garden, kitchen stores etc.

*Phase 4:*

*1948*
The National Health Service Act brought the majority of Hospitals under central control. St. Audry's and St. Clements formed a group with administrative control at St. Audry's. Known as Suffolk Mental Hospitals Management Committee. Patients now 1100 and 280 Staff.

*1950*
Dr. W. Brooks-Keith retired. Dr. I. J. Davies appointed.

*1957*
New sewing room and female O/T completed.

*1958*
Isolation Hospital renamed and refurbished and opened by H.R.H. The Duchess of Kent as Whitwell House.

*1959*
The Mental Health Act gave more protection to the patient with regular reviews and more informality in procedures. Patients now 1009 Staff 300. Farm buildings converted to Occ/Therapy, i.e. carpentry; bricklaying; ....

*c1960*
"Open Days" introduced. Patient Social Centre opened.
Over the past 30 years a great deal of money had been spent at St. Audry's to provide specialised services and on general improvements and modernisation. Redwald House now Early Treatment Unit. Dr. Davies retired: Dr. Rixon appointed (Consultant Psychiatrist)

*1964*
Chapel converted to use as art instruction unit.

*1968*
Dr. Rixon Physician Supt.

*Phase 5:*

*1972*
Amalgamated with Ipswich Group H.M.C. (General) to form the East Suffolk Health Authority. Dr. Rixon Consultant Psychiatrist.

*1974*
More re-organisation in the N.H.S.

* A Day Centre established for over 65s. (Burrows Unit)

Over 200 Volunteers take part in activities arranged by a Full Time Services Co-ordinator. Village Fund Raising Groups – Friends of the hospital – have been established.

Mini-Buses have been purchased over the years through voluntary subscriptions.

The Pathway Club has been set up in Woodbridge in conjunction with Social Services in Woodbridge. This provides preventative support and after care.

Local Schools and organisations visit the Hospital and Museum regularly; people also come on short and long term attachments.

Group Homes have been established in the community with some hospital based support.

Whitwell House has been re-opened to provide self-care hostel accommodation.

Burrows Unit – Intensive rehabilitation now Day Centre.

*1989*
317 patients. 319 staff approx.

*1993 (April)*
HOSPITAL CLOSED AFTER 226 YEARS
(167 as Psych. Hospital)
(51 as House of Industry)

**Early 20th century, inside one of the wards**

**...and showing a homely feel to the corridors, unusual for that time**

Village Specials during World War II

# Democracy in action

## The Parish Council

Melton Parish Council, under the Chairmanship of Mr Graham Laight, is aware of its corporate responsibility to serve the village and represent the interests of the community as a whole at grassroots level. "Open government" can aptly be applied to the operation and functions of Melton's Parish Council. In order to facilitate a better understanding of their work, they have been responsible for circulating to every household a copy of the Melton Parish Directory (Appendix 1). This gives a brief outline of the Council's duties and further, by listing every Councillor together with their addresses and telephone numbers, indicates that they are all readily available to listen, discuss and represent residents' interests and particular concerns. Members of the public are welcome to attend Council meetings (but not to participate), and times of meetings are not only printed in the Directory but are put on the Parish Council notice board outside the Parish Room.

The Clerk to the Council is the only paid member of the Parish Council, who, being a qualified accountant and familiar with the legalities of Council business, is a source of guidance and as such is of paramount importance. With a budget exceeding £11,000 good management is vital. However, it is salient that the Clerk has no voting powers and his presence at Council meetings is purely advisory (and only when requested).

The relationship of the Parish Council to the District and County Councils is clearly laid out in the Directory. In the past much confusion was often caused by residents simply not understanding which Council was responsible for a particular service. The local representatives on both the District and the Council are given, together with their addresses and telephone numbers, so that direct contact and consultation may be made by parishioners.

Many residents are concerned that the Parish Council is now little more than a talking shop and pressure group for local issues. However, it remains of vital importance that village concerns should at the outset be discussed publicly and representation, if need be, made either to the District or County Council, which is likely to have more clout than if undertaken by individual residents. The recent controversy over the proposed location of houseboats on the Deben at Melton occupied much Parish Council time, and it is significant that after their reservations were channelled to the District Council, the latter's plans were ultimately modified. In the case of the development of Melton Woods, however, which the Parish Council has consistently opposed, no such happy outcome has been forthcoming.

**April 27th, 1991**
**Mr Peter Hope's party at his home Red Towers, to commemorate his retirement after 33 years as Chairman of the Parish Council**

41  Aerial view of Melton Woods

St. Audry's Woods

Waterhead Lane

Melton Woods with trees marked
for felling, Spring 1994

St. Audry's Woods

**Thomas Churchyard: Lawyer's Wood Lane**

**Laura Churchyard: The Street**

"Lawyer's Wood Lane" reproduced by kind permission of
Christchurch and Ipswich Borough Museum and Gallery

# Melton Woods

The boundary of Melton with Ufford and Bredfield meanders through fields and by-ways. However the dividing line with Woodbridge is well defined by Pytches Road and continues across Melton Hill to the river; on old maps this is known as the Processional Way.

On the left hand side of Pytches Road going down the hill there was open country of cornfields, farmland, interspersed with woodland, sloping down to marsh meadows. Also in this area was an early brick kiln, and fragments of pottery have been found here over the years. On the opposite side of the road stood four windmills, shown on old maps of Woodbridge, overlooking Victoria Road. It is indicative of the amount of corn grown in this area that four mills should have had sufficient trade.

Thomas Pytches was a nineteenth century landowner, who gave his name to the road, which until recent times was only a narrow winding lane. He owned what is now Melton Grange Hotel, then a farmhouse known as Mount Pleasant. His estate included much of the surrounding woodland which was coppiced, as can be seen from the enormous stools of sweet chestnuts still visible.

Between the Wars development began on the western boundary, but it was not until after the Second World War that it spread to any extent across Bredfield Road, thereafter followed the building of estate after estate.

A beautiful valley, much appreciated by Bernard Barton, the famed nineteenth century Woodbridge poet was immortalised in his poem as "The Valley of Fern". His close friend, the accomplished artist Thomas Churchyard also knew the valley well and drew sketches from which etchings were made for publication. Timothy Leek was the landlord of the Green Man Inn, which was at the end of Love Lane, and held his renowned bullock sales in the adjoining meadow below the hill now carrying his name.

After the War, land was allocated for a school off Woods Lane, but this did not materialise and the area was bought and eventually planted up as an apple orchard. Bury Hill Estate, named after the big house built in 1898, was the first encroach-

ment of the Green Belt previously thought to be essential as a natural barrier between Melton and Woodbridge. The first phase of the development was built for, and occupied by, American servicemen and their families who were stationed at Bentwaters and Woodbridge USAF bases. The apple orchard was the next development, part of which became Orchard Close. Not long after, the Valley of Fern was advertised for housing and the steeply sloping side of the hill was cut into and beautiful mature oak, chestnut and ash trees were removed to make levels for houses to be built.

In Timothy Leek's water meadows the draining of the marsh, which was full of springs, began. Not surprisingly, the project became a far greater undertaking than had originally been anticipated. A deep ravine had to be dug through several feet of peat, yellow clay and blue boulder clay to tap the springs. Fossils, including those of whale rib-bones, sponges and copralite, were found; also twelfth century pottery fragments were excavated and identified by the Ipswich Archaeological Unit. The drainage project proved so complex that a Dutch firm was brought in to do the work. Higher up, sand to the depth of fourteen feet was removed and used to raise the level of the lower ground by the stream, in preparation for roads and services to be installed, and eventually for the houses. In all, some one hundred and eighteen houses were constructed and these became known as Melton Park Estate.

It was tragic to see the destruction of that beautiful pasture with its wealth of wild flowers – orchids, marsh marigolds, cowslips and many more. Trees, both young and mature were axed, despite their having many years of natural life ahead. Nothing was left. It was in 1974 that the first application to develop Melton Grange Woods was submitted. It was clear that, with so much already gone, the woods were vital to preserve anything of the original green belt. Visually, from the river, they provided a wooded skyline, offering an area rich in wildlife, where people could walk, relax and enjoy the environment – an abundance of spring flowers, notably snowdrops, primroses, wild daffodils and bluebells, the foliage of trees and bushes in the summer and autumn, with a number of ancient boundary oaks, providing all-year-round interest. Wildlife flourished. A pair of Muntjac deer and their faun were seen. Badgers were reputed to have a sett in this area, and a vixen with her cubs was a more common sight. Birdwatchers were rewarded with sightings of the three types of woodpeckers, tawny owl, kestrel, sparrowhawk, treecreepers, to name but a few. Nightingales competed with each other from thicket to thicket. Suddenly, and belatedly, people realised what was threatened, but in spite of much opposition over the next twenty years from both local and national pressure groups, planning permission was given for the woods to be developed and, significantly, this was against the advice of Melton Parish Council. Meltonians both old and new were heartbroken, not only for the loss to the environment but also, at a practical level, at the prospect of extra traffic from the houses in the Grange Woods and the adjoining Godfrey Wood, making a total of a hundred and ten houses which would come on flow to an already congested road system.

Melton is fortunate in having Burke's Wood and the playing field bequeathed for perpetuity by the late Sir Roland and Lady Burke, thus ensuring at least the rump of a natural break between Melton and Woodbridge. It is sad that the development came in by the backdoor and was the culmination of a slow but steady encroachment throughout the post-war period. Burke's Wood suffered from the hurricane of 1987 but much has since been replanted. In contrast, the Grange Woods were spared devastation. It is ironic that what was not damaged by the hurricane should be destroyed by the developers, who commenced felling Autumn 1994.

**Churchyard sketch of Fern Valley**

*The Valley of Fern*

*There is a lone valley, few charms can it number,*
*Compared with the lovely glens north of the Tweed;*
*No mountains enclose it where morning mists slumber,*
*And it never has echoed the shepherd's soft reed.*
*No streamlet of crystal, its rocky banks laving,*
*Flows through it, delighting the ear and the eye;*
*On its sides no proud forests, their foliage waving,*
*Meet the gales of the autumn or summer wind's sigh;*
*Yet by me it is prized, and full dearly I love it,*
*And oft my Steps thither I pensively turn;*
*It has silence within, heaven's proud arch above it,*
*And my fancy has named it the Valley of Fern.*

*Part II*

*Thou art changed, lovely spot! and no more thou displayest,*
*To the eye of thy votary, that negligent grace,*
*Which, in moments the saddest, the tenderest, the gayest,*
*Allured him so oft thy recesses to trace.*
*The hand of the spoiler has fallen upon thee,*
*And marr'd the wild beauties that deck'd thee before;*
*And the charms, which a poet's warm praises had won thee,*
*Exist but in memory, and bless thee no more.*
*The green, palmy fern, which the softest and mildest*
*Of summer's light breezes could ruffle, - is fled;*
*And the bright-blossom'd ling, which spread o'er thee her wildest*
*And wantonest hues, - is uprooted and dead.*

*Bernard Barton, c1817.*

## Melton Spring

*"There was a spring near a lane at the bottom of our garden (Melton old Rectory) where, as a lad I remember certain parishioners made daily journeys to drink water, and certainly either their faith or the water caused them to live long beyond the allotted span."*

*A. H. Harris, East Anglian Miscellany, 1949.*

Edgar Dowsing(1896 - 1984) wrote that he remembered drinking from the spring. The water was said to be good for rheumatism when drunk on an empty stomach. He had two great-aunts, one had great faith in the curative powers of Melton Spring and lived a careful and abstemious life, while the other took all the medication she could and was, in all respects, the opposite of her sister. Both lived to over 90, which cannot be regarded as a good case for the medicinal properties of the Melton waters! Mr Dowsing also tells the tale of a certain Rector, one of whose daughters was "a very poorly child, whose health gave great anxiety." However, upon being advised to drink the water from the Spring, she became stronger and eventually regained her health.

Local legend maintains that the curative powers of the Melton Spring date back to the Middle Ages and it is possible that this was the site of local pilgrimage, hence Holy Water Lane. In the early nineteeth century, Thomas Churchyard would make a drawing of it, and later, an etching for publication. Which is indicative of the beauty and popularity of the Spring.

MELTON SPRING.

**Thomas Churchyard's sketch of Melton Spring
engraved by J. Hawksworth, published in 1834**

45    Pupils of Class 3, Melton School, 1946

# Young Meltonians and their mentors

**Pupils and staff of Melton School, 1994**

Professor Aronson, the leading American physiologist, writes in his renowned "The Human Animal" that the way a community cares for its children and prepares them for adulthood is the best barometer of its general morale and confidence in the future. There are four schools catering for younger children listed in the current Melton Parish Directory, which certainly confirms the modern political jargon concerning the merits and need for choice in the community. Melton Primary School, whose present premises were opened in 1964, offers good modern facilities set in an ideal venue in the village centre. The attitude and enthusiasm of both staff and pupils is revealed in their contributions in this book.

The Church, under the able leadership of the Revs. Mark and Clare Sanders, offers a whole range of activities for all ages from 'tots to teens'. A cursory glance in "The Messenger" (St. Andrew's monthly magazine) confirms this, as does the high attendance at the Sunday Family Service.

# Challenge and change

Shortly after I arrived at Melton in September 1980 I was enrolled on a training course for Headteachers on the theme of 'The Role of the Head as an agent for change'. How prophetic that course turned out to be.

The last ten years have seen enormous changes in Primary Schools in general and Melton School in particular. At the time I took over, the closure of the school at Ufford was being mooted by the Local Education Authority but robustly resisted by the villagers of Ufford. The intended plan seemed to focus on the children from Ufford being moved to Melton which would have extended accommodation provided in the form of an additional mobile classroom. That particular scheme was subsequently dropped.

However, a few years later the whole of the education pattern in the Woodbridge area was extensively reviewed and the decision taken to close two Middle Schools and to revert to a Primary/Secondary system with Melton, along with other Primary schools in the Farlingaye Pyramid, catering for children in the 5-11 age group. In order to provide the additional facilities required for the extended age range, Melton School was extensively enlarged and re-modelled to provide accommodation for 240 children. Ufford school was to close and combine with us to enjoy the enhanced facilities. A merger - not a takeover.

The review also served to focus on Farlingaye (Woodbridge) as the catchment area High School for 10 Primary Schools, making it one of the largest school Pyramids in the County both in area and number of contributory feeder schools.

All this took place in the mid-eighties, coincident with the expansion of Melton itself. Almost overnight Melton appeared to change from a village with a village school to a more urban environment with a large Primary School in the middle.

Meanwhile the Education Reform Act was ensuring that both the curriculum and the way schools are managed were also to undergo significant changes. Schools were given their own budgets based on a formula common to all schools of a similar type through the County.

Melton was able to benefit from these developments. In 1990 we went into the Local Management of Schools with a newly refurbished and well equipped school, enabling us to look forward and not to have to replace and repair.

The National Curriculum has placed demands on staff and resources requiring almost constant change over the last five years. We have been well placed to meet those demands and can boast a well-stocked library, computers in every classroom, up to date equipment and, most important of all, a hardworking, dedicated and capable staff.

The school has had a quiet period following the closure of St Audry's Hospital and the twin bases at R.A.F. Bentwaters and R.A.F. Woodbridge. Our numbers dropped slightly and the staffing levels have had to be reduced.

As ever, changes are still taking place. Numbers of children being enrolled are rising rapidly; we will shortly have to increase the staffing levels, and, significantly, the latest directive from the Department for Education is only 166 pages thin!

*B. Swan, Headmaster*
*Melton County Primary School*

# Richard Bentham: 'A Father to the Parish' Headmaster of Melton School, 1893-1924

In 1893 Richard Bentham was chosen from 51 applicants to be the first headmaster of Melton Board School. He was 30 years of age, a short quick man, with reddish hair, bright eyes and a Lancashire accent.

After his successful interview he sat in the waiting-room at Melton Station wondering whether he had done right. It was a long way from his native North but he hoped that the country air would help his wife's health. It was also promotion from his deputy headship at Blackburn Furthergate Congregational School, a 'factory' school in the cotton mills area.

This was a time of change also for Melton school, which since 1845 had been under the aegis of the National Society for the Education of the Poor in the principles of the established Church. After several years of discussion between the local School Board and the National Society representatives it was decided by a convened meeting of Melton ratepayers to adopt the 1870 Education Act and so to transfer authority for its school to a school board.

At first it was decided to appoint Miss Bird as mistress of a girls' section and to appoint a master for the boys, but finally the school advertised for a Headmaster to be in charge of a Mixed School.

Miss Bird had taught at the school from 1864 but accepted the decision kindly. Richard treated her with friendly respect and insisted that she remain in the schoolhouse. His wife, Hannah, frequently visited her especially after her retirement in 1908. The late Peter Hope, of Red Towers, shared memories with Richard's grandchildren of making a sort of state visit to her, children and mothers, each summer holiday. Her grave is beside the Bentham family grave in the Old Church graveyard.

Richard's father had been a Primitive Methodist lay preacher involved in Sunday School teaching when that was the only form of education for the very poor. Richard thoroughly understood how upsetting the changes were for the Rector and National Society representatives and when the 1870 Education Act and 1902 Education Act were put into effect and the clergyman was no longer the centre of the school governing board, the

**Richard Bentham**

school managers applied each year for permission for him to teach Scripture to the children. However, the Inspectors were always full of praise for the manner in which the Melton children answered and the way in which the teaching had been related to their everyday lives.

The Morant code laid down guidelines for encouraging good moral behaviour in the children. Richard's maxims were "honesty at all times" and that "it did not matter what [work] you did as long as you did it with your whole heart". He believed also in sport as a great character builder and encouraged this in practical ways.

At the end of each day he would read for a couple of hours until midnight and then kneel down to say his prayers. On Good Friday he would always spend a quiet hour in prayer in the church.

Richard did a great deal of work for Melton Church but without pressurising his family of five sons and three daughters. On Sunday they did not have to accompany him to church but there were always several there proudly listening to their father reading the Lesson, unless Sir William Churchman preferred to do so. The latter with the Rector, Lawyer Wood of Wood's Lane and Richard Bentham, 'the father of the parish', formed an important quartet in Melton life. He was elected people's warden on many occasions and was the Choirmaster of a paid choir for several years. His grandchildren remember that he was treasurer because he brought home the Sunday collection, laid it out on the large dining/billiard table, counted it and took it to Friar's shop, who welcomed the change for the shop. Grandfather was given a cheque for banking at Woodbridge next day, and also bars of Fry's cream chocolate for the family – a welcome delicacy.

Richard arranged concerts in the school and also magic lantern shows – all for adults and in aid of church funds.

He became very much part of village life. He lived in two other houses before moving to Alma House and cottage on the other side of the driftway from Mile Stone cottage (one-time Post Office) in the centre of the village. The garden gate led into the playground. He had a study at the back of the house with a table strewn with papers on which he was working and, on two walls, books from floor to ceiling. It was here that people came to discuss their problems with him; to have help in completing income

tax forms or to have references written. Meals were frequently interrupted by villagers asking for his advice.

He was secretary/treasurer of the Doric Masonic Lodge, of which he wrote a history at the Lodge's request, to celebrate its centenary. In the last years of his life he was invited to Grand Lodge to receive special honours.

He had much to fit in with his ordinary school work, especially as there were so many inspections to ensure that the codes laid down by the 1902 Education Act were followed. He complained on one occasion to the school managers that it could not have been more inappropriate to have a P.E. inspection when the children's rest had been disturbed by three Zeppelin air raid alarms. He was pleased however that they had done well.

'Special subjects' were introduced by the Board of Education for which grants were available provided attendance was regular and the inspectors satisfied with the standard of work achieved. The Melton children travelled to Woodbridge for most of these subjects – 14 girls and one boy for cookery. The laundry class* was popular with the girls, who preferred it to a school holiday one Ascension Day (Melton School, being a Church School, always had Ascension Day as a special holiday). On one occasion the teacher failed to arrive, but word came to Richard who sent them a message that they were to return to school. The boys gardened, first on 'borrowed' land and then on land leased from the Churchmans. The soil was enriched in 1917 by the addition of 30 tons of horse manure from the Welsh Mounted Camp. It took the boys a whole day to barrow, and the headmaster a whole day to keep an eye on the boys, unobtrusively.

Experiments in education were being carried out. Melton volunteered for one in hygiene. A teacher, Mr. Knappett, disinfected the entire school with benzoline and izal. Ten days afterwards there was an official inspection of the result. (I wonder what the verdict was!)

Qualifications became important. One teacher and a drill instructor had to discontinue their service because they were not qualified under any Code Article. He was also told in 1904 that the monitor system was to be discontinued. Since the early days of Sunday school brighter pupils had been specially taught by the teacher and then passed on what they had learnt to a certain

---

* Melton laundry was an important employer of female staff, having a role of over 40 women and girls in the inter-war years.

number of other pupils. Richard had sometimes used his two monitors to give extra time to backward readers. He had them for several more years on the grounds that one teacher could not alone teach 50 infants, adding that infants under 4 should not be admitted to the school and infants under 5 should only be admitted if specially sanctioned by the school managers. At this time he had 8 or 9 under-fives.

There had always been pupil teachers to help fill gaps in the teaching staff until they were of age to study for their qualifying exams. Now regulations were stiffened. A pupil teachers' report book had to be maintained. Daughter Maud remembers that the pupil teachers came to the house for her father to help them prepare the next day's lessons and that he helped them in class also. She remembers particularly Kate Budinger and Dolly Holmes. His two daughters, Ida and Dorothy, also became pupil teachers at times when he was in dire straits. They returned to their studies at Leiston Girls' School when staffing was sufficient. Once when Woodbridge Council School closed for a week he was successful in his application to borrow their two pupil teachers for that time.

His school was as successful as other schools in the number of scholarships obtained to Woodbridge School, to Mills Grammar School Framlingham, to the Ipswich Girls' High School and to Leiston. He had to work extremely hard for his good results because there were frequent epidemics which resulted in the school being closed by the Medical Officer of Health for several weeks at a time. On one occasion he managed to obtain permission to open the school for one day in the midst of the closure. He examined the whole school in reading, writing and arithmetic on that day and entered the results in the report book.

He constantly tested the Standards in those subjects and took the classes himself if they were below par, returning to his own class when they were satisfactory again.

When he retired as headmaster he was immediately elected to the board of school managers. He had received two presentations for his work in the school and the parish, one in 1917 and one in 1924 on his retirement. At his death the Chairman of the Managers referred to his long experience and expert advice "which made him in this work, as in so many other offices which he filled in Melton, invaluable".

A few months before his death, near his 80th birthday, he was made a presentation for his many interests: his work as Clerk to the Parish Council, for encouraging the setting up of a club and reading room for the lads in the Parish Room and for being, as the Rev. Hurd said in his funeral address, 'a father to the parish'.

*Miss Barbara Pratt*
*Woodbridge*
*Granddaughter of Richard Bentham (1863-1943)*

# Miss Dee
## Teacher, 1921-1962

"I joined the teaching staff of Melton Council School on February 1st, 1921, when Mr. Richard Bentham was nearing his retirement. The number on the school roll was 120 divided into four sections: Infants, Juniors, Intermediates and Seniors. Scholars were admitted at five years of age and remained until they became fourteen.

The classes were arranged in standards according to attainment chiefly in the three R's (Reading, Writing and Arithmetic). Discipline was strict and timetables were closely observed. The school year ended on March 31st, and during that month each child was given a test issued by the East Suffolk Education Authority and the individual results were recorded in books by fixing the examination papers each year in the appropriate places, thus ensuring a continuous record of each scholar's attainment. In addition, Mr. Bentham, who was an able elocutionist, tested each class in reading aloud and reciting. He was also a keen sportsman and cricket and football were played by the senior boys, and netball by the girls. Swimming, in the river, was also included during the summer term.

May 24th, Empire Day, was always observed with lessons connected with the growth of the Empire and in the history and formation of the Union Jack during the morning; in the afternoon was the annual sports day.

At this time radio was in the experimental stage, and broadcasting during the day was just beginning. Mr. Bentham had acquired a set with a loudspeaker, and it was a great attraction for the children to listen-in after school hours. The reception at this stage was varied and often very disappointing.

School gardens were cultivated by the senior boys and each year prizes were given by Sir William Churchman for the best plots. The school also had a National Savings Bank to which many parents contributed for their children's future needs.

School meals were not provided, but Mrs. Sullivan, who was a manager of the school, brought cocoa and milk for those scholars who came from a distance and had to bring packed lunches, and the staff in turn saw to the making of the drinks.

The infants were taught in a separate building which was the original school. It consisted of a large room arranged in tiers for seating at dual desks with a large space left for activity, and a smaller room which was used as a store for school materials. The cloakrooms were each fitted with three washbasins and running water. Toilets were outside and reached by a covered passage.

The school was regularly inspected by H.M.I. from the Board of Education for secular subjects and by a clergyman of the Church of England and a minister of the non-conformist church for religious knowledge.

Mr. Marshall succeeded Mr. Bentham in 1924. The general outlook was very similar regarding the discipline and curriculum, but a few months later Mr. Marshall left Melton to become head of Wickham Market Council School and Mr. Brewster from Lowestoft took charge of Melton until, after a short stay, he left the profession to join a publishing firm. Thus within 2-3 years we had three headmasters, which was in many respects not easy for either the teaching staff or pupils, particularly since Mr. Bentham had been head for so many years and had been highly respected throughout the community.

Mr. Blake, also from Lowestoft, was then appointed to Melton. Under Mr. Blake's authority, school uniforms were adopted and, with the cooperation of parents, gradually all pupils wore navy blazers and school badges. Girls wore navy gym slips and white blouses and all had black and yellow striped ties. Strict attention was given to cleanliness and general appearance, and courtesy and polite manners were insisted upon.

Singing was Mr. Blake's favourite subject and the school choir was formed. Concerts were frequently given, and a piano was bought for school use, as previously the only available instrument was a very old harmonium.

Mr. Blake left to become headmaster of Trimley School in 1932, and Mr. Capp from Friston was appointed to Melton. The pupils at this time were re- arranged in age groups irrespective of attainment, and the former "standards" became "classes", each arranged in groups of similar ability. The general trend in education at this time was for teachers to teach subjects in which they were interested throughout the school in addition to the basic work of their respective classes. This arrangement proved both interesting and successful, and handwork, art, music, dramatic work, physical training etc. benefited.

Many urgent necessities were bought for school use through efforts in concerts and dramatics. To further musical training percussion instruments were obtained for the younger children, a radio to enable broadcast lessons to be followed, and a cinematograph for illustrating geography, history and nature lessons. During this time the installation of electricity throughout the building was much appreciated.

The school choir regularly entered the competitions arranged by the Woodbridge Musical Festival, and a highlight of their performance was reached when Roger Quilter, the renowned Suffolk composer[*], came from the audience and congratulated them on the rendering of his composition "Blossom Time".

In 1937 the coronation of King George VI was celebrated by the children and staff uniting in the performance of their original play "Homage" on the meadow near the school. A year later, in 1938, the younger children competed in the County Drama Festival, and secured second place for the play "Rumpelstiltskin". Country dancing was also eagerly contested at the Folk Dancing Festivals. Under Mr. Capp's leadership each teacher was encouraged to use their own initiative in the subjects taught, and this proved highly successful.

In addition to the foregoing forms of study, school educational tours were arranged and journeys undertaken to see the various places of interest in London, e.g. The Tower, Houses of Parliament, St. Paul's Cathedral, Hampton Court etc. and to other places within reasonable travelling distance.

The effects of war were felt in school life from 1940. Evacuation from crowded cities, fear of bombing and threats of gas became realities of our daily life. Each child had their gas-

[*] His sister Mrs Vivian lived at Foxborrow Hall and had a great interest in village life, as did her son, the late Major Miller.

mask on their desk and regular practice was needed in using the mask speedily. Many lessons were missed as time was spent in the dug-outs (not always to the sorrow of some pupils). Economies in materials also were felt and newspapers were now used for painting paper, while pictures were also painted, in mural style, on the walls. School meals were instituted and these were taken in an empty house in company with schools evacuated from Grays (Essex) and West Ham.

Mr. Capp was appointed headmaster of Halesworth Senior School in 1940, and Mr. Keeble from Peasenhall took charge of Melton. For the next five years the war raged and every school had to work under trying circumstances. The chief variations were fund raising for prisoners of war, and efforts to promote investment in National Savings. When the celebrations for peace had finished normal routine was resumed as material supplies improved and classrooms became less crowded when evacuees returned home.

In 1955 the school became a primary school catering for pupils up to 11+, and the senior scholars entered Farlingaye Secondary Modern, Woodbridge, or boys passing the 11+ went to Woodbridge Grammar (now Woodbridge School), and girls to Mills Grammar School in Framlingham.

When Mr. Keeble retired from the profession in 1951 and Mr. Bruce was appointed headmaster of the school, the general trend in all schools altered. A free and easy discipline was general, and the method of teaching changed. The "Project Method" was advocated instead of direct lessons. This proved rewarding both for staff and pupils when carefully directed. The staff at Melton studied the method at several venues including Lowestoft and Welwyn Garden City.

By this method a topic was selected and research carried out by the student, either individually or in small groups. The approach was as broad as possible, thus incorporating many subjects that were formerly isolated. For instance in the study of "Bread", the geography included the wheat growing area of East Anglia and the overseas countries, e.g. Canada. The development of grinding and baking bread through the ages needed history study; while keen observation was encouraged to follow the work of the farmer, miller and baker. Step-by-step booklets were made by the pupils and illustrated during art lessons, and measuring and counting were associated with arithmetic lessons. The crowning point was the visit to the local bakery, assisting in the making of bread, weighing the flour and salt, measuring the liquid, setting the yeast and watching the electrical mixer at work. Later everyone saw the dough kneaded and put in the oven to bake. At the third visit the finished loaves were ready and stacked for sale.

Other topics of interest were the study of wool and weaving, with a visit to view the looms and materials at Lavenham, "Iron and its uses" involved viewing the work at Pearce's Ironworks at Bredfield, and the work of the nurse, with demonstrations by the local district nurse in bandaging,

Another very interesting project proved to be the study of the River Deben, from its source at Debenham to its estuary at Felixstowe. Details of various types of boats and ships from the Viking vessels, the wind controlled ships and barges to modern yachts and motor vessels, provided a source of valuable information for art and history lessons, while the transporting of grain and coal by barges was a link with geography in the wider study of imports and exports.

During the 1960s preparation for the new school building began, but my service ended in 1962 after 41 years of very happy association with managers, headmasters, parents and children of Melton."

*Written in 1978 by Miss H.E. Dee (1894-1991)*

**Teaching staff at Melton School, 1948**
**Standing - Mrs Reeves, Mr Keeble, Miss Grimwood, Mr Grove,**
**Seated - Miss Ward, Miss Dee**

# *Pupils at Melton School*, 1948

**Infants**

**Juniors**

**Seniors**

Melton Old Primary School

# REUNION PARTY

at The School Hall
New Primary School, Melton

on Friday, 27th November, 1987
6.30  —  9 p.m.

**Miss Ida Ward, Miss Messenger and Miss Hilda Dee**

**Mrs Hazel Green talking to Miss Dee,
Miss Ward and Miss Messenger in the background**

# The Teacher's day

For most of the teaching staff the day begins shortly after 8.00 a.m. when they arrive to prepare classrooms and resources for the day's work. Tasks may include collecting together equipment for a science activity, photocopying work-sheets, setting out apparatus, putting up and labelling displays, choosing a selection of books from the school library for use in the classroom and so on. At 9.05 a.m. the teacher on duty blows the whistle and the children line up by classes on the playground ready to come in to school.

There are seven classes arranged by age, the youngest being a little under 5 years old whilst the oldest are 11. As in all other primary schools, the children are divided into Key Stage 1 (age 4-7) and Key Stage 2 (7-11). Registration and the marking of the dinner book are brief affairs and soon the day's work begins.

As required by the National Curriculum the children study 10 subjects, with a greater proportion of time being devoted to the "core" subjects of English, Maths and Science. The other subjects taught are History, Geography, Technology, Art, Music, P.E. and R.E., and each member of the teaching staff has an oversight of one or more of the curriculum areas throughout the whole school.

Generally the children are organised into groups and may be engaged in a variety of different activities related to the same subject. One group may be working on a practical task with an adult (classroom ancillary or volunteer helper) whilst the teacher supervises the remaining groups. As children complete tasks some rotation will take place or they may move on to a supplementary activity. Classroom furniture is arranged so that children sit in groups of 6 or 8 around tables, keeping their books and other belongings in trays stored in trolley units in the classroom. Each classroom has a blackboard, a book area for browsing and quiet reading and an activity area equipped with a sink. In some classrooms coats are stored on pegs in the room, and in others there is a small cloakroom immediately outside the classroom. Children operate computers and tape recorders regularly and are confident in their use; T.V. programmes or tape/C.D. recordings are often used in a variety of ways for teaching purposes.

Assembly takes place every day just before morning play. On most days the whole school assembles in the hall for this, but on Wednesday classes meet together in smaller groups for 'infant' and 'unit' (2 classes) assemblies. The Friday assembly each week is a merit assembly when one child from each class is awarded a merit badge to wear for one week. Such badges are gained for a variety of reasons - good work, improved effort, keeping the classroom tidy, helping a new child to settle into school, producing an outstanding piece of written or art work and so on.

The children's work is constantly monitored and assessed by their teachers and at present SATs (standard assessment tasks) are conducted in English and Maths at the end of Key Stage 1 when the children are about 7 years old. The school has a topic programme which all children follow throughout the school and work is carefully planned by the staff to ensure that a balance is maintained between subjects.

Lunchtime begins at 12.05 for the Key Stage 1 children and at 12.15 for those in Key Stage 2. Meals are cooked on the premises and some children have a school lunch. The remainder bring a packed lunch each day which they eat sitting at tables in the hall for most of the year, but outside on the grass on warm summer days. The lunch 'hour' continues until 1.15 p.m. and during this time the children are able to play outside. In dry weather they are able to use the field and much enjoy the extra space that this provides. They are supervised by a number of 'dinner ladies' during this play and the teachers use the time for meetings, marking the morning's work, setting up activities for the afternoon and a multitude of other tasks, as well as finding a few minutes to eat their own lunch.

The school has a uniform which all children wear – grey shorts/trousers/skirts with white or grey shirts/blouses and green or grey jumpers or cardigans. Many children wear a school sweatshirt which has the school logo printed on it. In summer the girls wear green and white checked dresses. For P.E. lessons the children change into navy shorts and white T shirts and in winter the older ones bring in tracksuits which they wear for games activities outside.

**Melton School, 1965**

During their time at the school the children take part in a variety of visits connected with their work ranging from a walk around Melton looking at shapes, to a full day visit to a London museum. The oldest pupils in Year 6 may also take part in a residential visit to a P.G.L. activity centre where they sample a variety of outdoor pursuits such as pony trekking, abseiling, canoeing etc.

Afternoon school is organised in a similar way to the morning, but with only the Key Stage 1 children taking part in an afternoon playtime, and at 3.30 p.m. all children leave to go home. On some days groups of children may stay behind to take part in a variety of after school clubs such as netball, choir, short tennis etc.

For the teaching staff the day continues for a considerable time after this. Each Monday they attend a staff meeting and on other evenings they may be mounting work and putting up new display boards, marking work, testing out a newly purchased

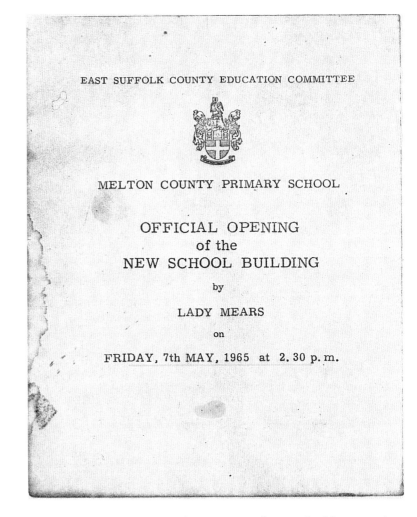

EAST SUFFOLK COUNTY EDUCATION COMMITTEE

MELTON COUNTY PRIMARY SCHOOL

OFFICIAL OPENING
of the
NEW SCHOOL BUILDING

by

LADY MEARS

on

FRIDAY, 7th MAY, 1965 at 2.30 p.m.

computer programme, setting up a new 'interest' table, returning to storage equipment or books their children no longer need, attending one of the many 'twilight' (i.e. 4.30-6.30) courses on aspects of education, filling in children's records or undertaking another of the multitude of tasks that are always there waiting to be done; not to mention planning tasks and groups for the following day when it will all begin again!

*Helen Lynch, June 1994*

# From the School Log Book

*Board of Education*
*Local Education Authority: Suffolk (East)*
*School: Melton Council No. 141*
*Inspected on 7th and 8th November 1935*
*Report by H.M.I. Mr. W.K. Spencer*

This School is doing very good work. The Head Master*, who took charge about three years ago, directs the activities of the children with much methodical skill and forethought, and is assisted by a loyal and capable staff. In spite of being in charge of a class his oversight is close and detailed, but at the same time he gives the teachers wide scope and makes good use of their special abilities.

English and Arithmetic are up to the standard usually found in well taught schools of this size and type. Good work is expected and good work is, therefore, obtained.

In the Senior Classes the Head Master tries to make up for the lack of Handicraft and Domestic Science by (a) the teaching of Gardening to both boys and girls and (b) by lessons in Bookcrafts. The Garden is situated at a distance** and is therefore more difficult to cultivate than if it surrounded the school. The standard of teaching is, however, good, and the garden, containing vegetables and fruit for utility, and flowers and a lawn for beauty, does credit to both Head Master and children. The lessons on Bookcrafts, besides giving exercises in measuring and manipulation, are useful in the provision of portfolios and book covers for use throughout the school. The Handwork done by the Infants is varied and specially worthy of note.

Music and Art reach a pleasing standard. The School usually does well in the Musical Festival held in the district.

Good use is made of the somewhat limited space in school and playground. The Infants have one of the larger rooms to allow for their special activities. Around the rooms are drawings and diagrams, evidence of a wide and interesting curriculum.

* Mr Capp   ** In New Road, now Saddlemaker's Lane

**The Old Schoolhouse**

**Melton Old School**

# School pictures

**Football Team, 1954**

| | |
|---|---|
| Back | Michael Crane, John Kersey, Raymond Horrocks, Michael Friend, Peter Hawes, Kenneth Orford, Mr. Robinson |
| Middle | David Kersey, David Wade, Brian Fisk, Michael Buck, Ian Smith |
| Front | Michael Humphrey, Charles O'Connor |

**In the school gardens, 1952**

Senior girls, 1952

Back    Miss Grimwood, Margaret Stone, Pat Griffiths,
        Muriel Bington, Margaret Grove
Front   Doris Garvie, Doreen King, Eileen Leek,
        Daphne Evans, Thurl Osborne,

Netball Team, 1954

Back    Jane Freeman, Nancy Proctor,
        Janet Milldown, Rosalind Sexton
Front   Beryl Copping, Christine Turner
        Kathleen O'Connor

# The Melton Young People's Fellowship 1946-62

For nearly two decades the YPF dominated social life for many of the younger Meltonians. Its wide ranging activities (Appendix 3) confirm one of its earliest successes and its continuing appeal. Its very existence relied upon the inspiration of the late Rev. Richard Hurd, who recognised the need for such an organisation in the village (the dearth of social activities for young people after the Second World War was emphasised by the return of many ex-servicemen, plus the continuing economic and social deprivation). He had the gift of being able to delegate responsibility to others, combined with a sense of enthusiasm which was clearly manifested during the YPF's early years. In many respects both Mr Hurd and the YPF were ahead of their time. By its constitution, although loosely under the auspices of the church (as confirmed by the list of activities) it was in no way dominated by or affiliated to the Church of England. Members were not expected to attend church regularly, or to be necessarily involved in Christian activities. It was, as one member put it, a means of showing practical Christianity, care and concern for fellow young Meltonians.

The programme of events very much reflected the local talent that existed within the YPF at a given time. Thus it was no accident that with such personalities as Arthur Smith, Roy Burrows, Marian Davis and the late Bob Wiffin, amateur dramatics should play an active role. Sports also figured prominently, as many members were keen to be involved in such activities. By talking to many past members and studying the minutes, the many interests of the organisation can be clearly seen.

The establishment of the YPF was a courageous undertaking, but its disbandment in 1962 can equally be justified. Sadly, over the previous three to four years support for organised events had tailed off and the overall age of members had increased without attracting younger members. The YPF is still held in high regard by Meltonians, and this was demonstrated when a reunion was held in 1980. Many conversations with Meltonians have included reminiscences concerning the YPF, and a general feeling that a vacuum still remains in village life after thirty years.

October 1946  YPF formed

| | | |
|---|---|---|
| 1946 | Wed. November 6th | YPF Social in Infants School after Church Service |
| | Mon. November 11th | Meeting at The Rectory to put YPF on proper footing |
| | Wed. December 4th | Social after Church Service |
| | Sat. December 14th | Social |
| 1947 | Sat. January 11th | Church Service/Meeting & Social |
| | Sat. January 18th | New Year Party |
| | Sat. February 15th | Church Service/Meeting & Social |
| | Sat. February 22nd | Church Service & Social |
| | Sat. March 22nd | Social |
| | Mon. April 14th | YPF Week commenced |
| | Tues. April 15th | Dance |
| | Weds. April 16th | Full dress rehearsal for concert |
| | Thurs. April 17th | Concert |
| | Fri. April 18th | ditto |
| | Sat. April 19th | Social (Draw raised over £40) |
| | Sun. April 20th | Special Church Service (YPF read lessons) |
| | Thurs. May 1st | Invited to attend Parish Meeting to decide what to do with Sports Fund Money (£500) |
| | Fri. May 9th | Took boys for Cricket Practice on Sir Roland's meadow* |
| | Fri. May 16th | ditto |
| | Sun. May 18th | YPF in force supported Youth Church Service led by Lord Alistair Graham |
| | Mon. May 19th | Hiking Section over Sutton Heath |
| | Tues. May 27th | Tennis at Sullivan's (Hermitage) |
| | Fri. May 30th | Arranged Cricket match |
| | Tues. June 10th | Tennis Tournament |
| | Thurs. June 26th | Tennis at Melton Mead** |

* Later Melton Playing Field   ** Home of Sir Roland Burk

| 1947 | Mon. June 30th | Cycle ride |
| (contd) | Tues. July 1st | Tennis at Sir Roland's |
| | Fri. July 11th | Cricket match versus ATC. Won. Played at St Audry's Hospital |
| | Fri. July 18th | Cricket match versus Sea Scouts. Won. |
| | Mon. Sept 15th | Sub Committee 7 and Main Committee 8 working on constitution |
| | Sat. Oct 25th | 1st Birthday Party |
| | Sun. Oct 26th | Church Service |
| | Sat. Nov 1st | Social |
| | Sat. Nov 22nd | Social |
| | Sat. Dec 6th | Social |
| | Sat. Dec 13th | Dance |
| | Sat. Dec 19th | Xmas Draw (over 1000 tickets sold at 3d each) |
| | Sat. Dec 20th | Carol Service followed by Club Night |
| | Sat. Dec 31st | Dance |

| 1956 | Sun. Jan 8th | Hockey versus Cowells. Lost 0-9 |
| | Sat. Jan 14th | New Year Party |
| | Sat. Feb 4th | Social |
| | Fri. Mar 2nd | Club Night |
| | Sun. Mar 4th | Hockey versus Leiston. Draw 1-1 |
| | Sat. Mar 10th | Social |
| | Sun. Mar 18th | Hockey versus Leiston. Lost 1-7 |
| | Sat. Mar 24th | Club Night |
| | Sun. Mar 25th | Hockey versus Saxmundham. Lost 4-5 |
| | G/Fri Mar 30th | Did Passion Play at Church |
| | Sat. Apr 14th | Jumble Sale |
| | Weds. Apr 25th | Treasure Hunt |
| | Sun. Jun 3rd | Church Service |
| | Sat. July 21st | Flower Show (invited Eaton Y.C.) & Arts and Crafts Exhibition |
| | Sat. Oct 6th | AGM |
| | Thurs. Oct 25th | Visit to Felixstowe to see "Quaker Girl" |
| | Sat. Oct 27th | 10th Birthday Party |
| | Sat. Nov 10th | Club Night |
| | Fri. Nov 23rd | YPF show. "Playgoers" – "Before the Morning" – "Monkey's Paw" |
| | Sat. Nov 24th | Second night of show |
| | Weds. Nov 28th | Social |
| | Sun. Dec 2nd | Hockey versus E&R Howards. Draw 0-0 |
| | Sat. Dec 11th | YPF Sale of Work (Opened by Lady Blanche Cobbold) |
| | Mon. Dec 17th | Carols at St Audry's |
| | Tues. Dec 18th to Mon. Dec 24th | Carolling around the village £16.0.0. (Record) |

Melton Young People's Fellowship, Christmas Social, 1955

## Historic Pageant by the school children, May 1937

The weather interfered with the Melton celebrations to the extent that the sports programme was postponed until 6 p.m. on the night of Whit Monday. In addition the heavy rains necessitated the teas having to be served indoors, children (170) in the school, and adults (474) in the Parish Room and the garage opposite.

The specially arranged Church services for Sunday and Coronation Day were attended by large congregations.

The first item on the official programme was a Pageant of the Empire by the school children, who made a very picturesque, colourful and realistic show of historical events from the time of Queen Boadicea. A lovely Queen (Fay Upson) led the way, and as the procession marched to its appointed place, the various characters came forward to recite their lines and the company sang appropriate songs. It was felt that the display was worthy of the occasion, and the spectators, who had assembled in large numbers despite the weather, expressed their appreciation of the efforts of the teaching staff and children very warmly.

The Sports then began, but after fourteen events had been completed, the rain made further progress impossible. Tea was then served early, and many who lived at a distance from the centre of the village remained behind to hear a Variety Entertainment in the Parish Room and by so doing produced the sight of a full house an hour before the appointed time of starting. The entertainment, which included sketches, songs, dancing, violin solos, and recitations, continued until 11.15 p.m., a break at 8 o'clock affording the opportunity of hearing the King's speech. It was a splendid entertainment, and reflected great credit on the organisers and participants. It was arranged primarily for old age pensioners, who occupied the seats of honour and were supplied with liberal refreshments at the interval.

Coronation mugs used at tea were presented to all children below working age, and oranges provided by a generous supporter, although the handing out of these was not possible owing to the postponement of the Sports.

Coronation tins of tea will be sent to the aged and infirm who were unable to be present.

*Woodbridge Reporter, May 13th 1937.*

**Melton's own play "Homage", performed by the children, *assisted* by *selected* adults (Nurse Powling in uniform, and Miss Dee).**

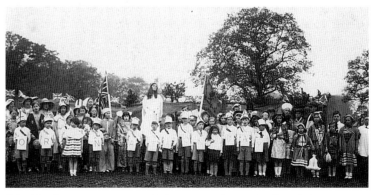

**Miss Fay Upson was the central character as Britannia. (Rainfall on Coronation Day necessitated a second performance on the following day.)**

# Scouts and Guides

## 1st Melton Scout Troop

I joined the scouts in 1950, at the age of eleven. As for the previous history of the Melton scouts, my knowledge is a bit sketchy, but I do know that the previous rector, the Rev. R. Hurd, had run the troop for a number of years.

When I started, there were two patrols, these being the Kestrels (my patrol) and the Eagles. The scoutmaster at that time was Barry Mortimer, who lived with the Skoulding family in Station Road. He was assisted by Maurice Smith and Trevor Newson.

Whilst our normal Monday evening meetings were held in the Parish Room, our activities were often in the open air – usually at Leeks Hills. Thus in Summer we frequently met at the house of Bob Tile, an active supporter, whose house was conveniently situated. If we got there early we were able to listen to Dick Barton on the wireless before the meeting started!

Our time was taken up with getting through the Tenderfoot test before the Second Class and individual interest badges. I did obtain my cooking badge, but forget what I had to do for it, except that one of our delicacies was the "twist" which consisted of a mixture of flour and water, wound round a stick and 'cooked' over an open fire. I think the main attraction was the smoky taste. Of more practical use was first aid instruction, given by, I believe, a member of the St. John's Ambulance.

Sometimes we had what we called "wide games", which, as I recall, usually meant laying a trail for the other patrol and ambushing them if they were clever enough to end up near where we were waiting. Great fun!

The highlight of the year, however, was the annual camp. In 1950 we went to St. Osyth, Essex, where we learnt all about sleeping on hard ground, digging (and using) latrines and putting up tents. We used bell tents, which meant that our feet tended to meet in the middle against the pole. We all took our bikes so we were able to visit Clacton and other surrounding places. (I think nearly all of us boys had bicycles in those days.) The following two years, 1951 and 1952, we camped at Oulton Broad, near Lowestoft, and this venue I found as exciting if not more so. In retrospect I realise how much planning went into these annual camps. For instance, while at Oulton Broad, visits to Norwich, Great Yarmouth and Lowestoft were organised. We were not just left to our own devices at these times. We had conducted tours of local places of interest, including factories. One year we visited the large cooperative food-processing plant at Lowestoft. The next year we went round the coach-building works. We met Mr Mobbs, the farmer on those land we camped, and he showed us around his farm, explaining the work carried out, making us aware of environmental issues (unusual at this time). On a more social note, we went to shows at the Sparrow's Nest outside Lowestoft, took trips on the Broads, and one year watched the speedboat races.

Sometimes the patrol would go camping by itself (no scoutmasters) for a weekend. We usually went down by the river towards Ufford, and our other activities were supplemented by swims in the river (not all we scouts could swim, but our parents remained blissfully unaware of possible tragedy). On one occasion I remember our patrol pitched their bell tent over a large hollow in the ground. This was fine until a cloudburst during the night, when the area within the tent rapidly became a miniature lake!

Our standard of fieldcraft must have been quite high, as in 1952 or 1953 we were runners-up (out of about 40) in the county camping competition at Shrubland Park near Ipswich.

The Melton troop was however in some difficulty from about 1953, because of the shortage of leaders and the general decline in numbers. Eventually, Jack Cook, who lived in Station Road and who had been a scouter some years before, became the scoutmaster.

It was no longer possible to arrange an annual camp, although we did have one or two weekends at Foxborough Hall. Instead, in 1954, I was able to join the Kesgrave scouts at their camp at Gilwell Park, near Chigwell, Essex. The following year there were sufficient Melton scouts to form a patrol as we joined the Kesgrave scouts for their camp at Herringfleet, near Lowestoft.

After that I left the Melton Scouts, although I did for a time attend meetings at Kesgrave, where they had a patrol of Senior Scouts. Later, in the autumn of 1957, I returned to help Jack Cook in the running of the troop, but my association with them finally ceased when I entered the Army the following year.

*David Blake*

## Guides

Melton Guide Company offers an opportunity for 10-15 year olds to develop corporate and individual self-reliance skills. They meet once a week during school term and almost all the twenty-five or so members live within the village confines. The morale of the group is high, and far exceeds its numbers, which is confirmed by the wide range of activities on offer. The development of practical skills such as first-aid remains at the core of guiding. Further, working together in patrols offers an opportunity to develop leadership skills. The culmination of this and the annual highlight for most guides is the summer camp. Independent living with one's peers, away from parental supervision, and the excitement of sleeping under canvas means almost 100% attendance. Participation in community activities, such as St Andrew's 125th Anniversary Festival, is encouraged and helps to 'show the flag' at a local level. Certainly the Melton company has moved away from a more traditional middle class image, but continues to hold respect within the community.

**The Brownies on duty!**
**Joyce Lankester's wedding**

**1962, the Brownies under the leadership of the late Miss**
**Rachel Burke (right) assisted by Joyce Lankester.**

## Children's views of Melton

Discipline and respect for one's elders and 'betters' were accepted especially by the village child - until well after the Second World War. I remember from my own childhood spent in Melton, that while we had moved on from the Victorian ideal of being seen but not heard, we were careful and selective to whom we openly expressed our own views and opinions. In complete contrast the contemporary child is not encumbered in this way; he (or she) is far more confident and spontaneous, and this leads to a much more inquiring and questioning attitude to life.

From a series of exercises set at Melton County Primary School a much clearer picture of how the children perceive Melton has become evident. Younger children listed the salient aspects of Melton life, which included: "lovely and beautiful views" of the Deben and surrounding countryside, "family, friends and friendly people", living in the community, the "shops and pubs", the size of the village (which varied from 'large' to 'small'!). The Church and 'Mark' the Rector were recurring points mentioned, as was the small number of children today who have any concept of the traditional idea of a village with a focal point and boundaries, which was part of my consciousness in my early days here fifty years ago. Types of houses "old, new, small and large, and a mixture!" – "the playing field, river, woods" as places of recreation were also frequently listed. Some children were moved by the natural beauty of the whole area - trees, flowers, and wildlife.

The older and more articulate child describes Melton as a "good place to live", with "friendly, caring and supportive family, friends and neighbours", and with a "large modern school, set in its own extensive grounds". The more discerning think the pubs and roads could be quieter, but according to another 11 year old there are "lots of things to do, with such periodic excitements as the visiting circus" (which had been based recently on the Melton Playing field). One 11 year old makes the point that the shops provide for virtually all the needs of life, within walking distance. Already this age group are concerned with environmental issues: the main road passing through Melton is for many a source of excitement, but also concern (danger) plus 'dirt' and noise; Melton woods "sadly are to be chopped down to build more houses". Another senior pupil pinpoints "Melton County Primary School as the centre of the village".

One 10 year old (on May 11th 1994 precisely 10 years, 5 months and one day old!) makes the profound observation: "Some minor things are very irritating in Melton, but after a while one gets used to them". A statement by another child is germane to the idea of the advantages for Meltonians of all ages: "Melton is one of the best places to live, with everything one needs nearby".

"Our postcode is Melton, Woodbridge" emphasises how little the traditional boundaries of the village mean to the child of today. Television, and increased mobility, have resulted in a change in the contemporary child's perception of village life. It means that they are nationally far more 'cosmopolitan' and no longer inward-looking.  The village provides few families with employment, let alone all the necessities of life. It is a base (giving, we hope, a secure foundation) from which to travel. East Anglia, the U.K., Europe and beyond are all taken as the norm.

Burk's Wood, replanted in 1991
after the 1987 hurricane

Ancient woodland soon to be sorely missed by young and old alike.

69    **Sheep crossing Wilford Bridge, by Thomas Churchyard**

# The Lamb Sale

The annual lamb sale held on the Church Meadow was synonymous with the Bloss family, who moved to the village around 1860. The family originated from the Dennington area, where they were well-known and respected as cattle farmers, drovers and cattle dealers. Melton was an ideal site for all three trades, which were closely inter-related. The village was an important route centre, river transport from Melton Docks and quay flourishing well within living memory. Wilford Bridge, the lowest bridging on the Deben, gave easy access to the coastal land with its traditional sheep walks. The main London to Yarmouth road passed through the village, and, from 1859, the railway with its well-appointed station and large goods yards was ideally suited for transporting cattle. In addition, three weekly cattle markets were within easy droving distance: Monday at Wickham Market (later at Campsea Ashe) Tuesday at Ipswich and Thursday at Woodbridge – all three required no overnight layering (giving security and grazing for a limited period, often overnight). Added to these strategic advantages, the land owned and rented by the Blosses in Melton was used for resting (layering and longer) and the fattening of stock.

Throughout late spring and early summer a series of lamb sales were held throughout East Anglia. Lambs bred and reared on the "light" coastal land were sold to "heavy" inland farmers, who fattened them over the winter months. Melton lamb sale became traditionally the big one, and from 1912 until the mid-1950s its venue was the Church Meadow next to St. Andrew's New Church in the centre of the village, the site of the present St. Andrew's Place. It was held about three-quarters of the way through this period, at the end of June or the first week of July. Until the post-War period most farms were mixed. Thus, the sale of lambs gave an important cash input at a time when finances were at their lowest in the run-up to harvest. Vendors would walk their stock carefully as they were concerned to ensure that their lambs arrived in prime condition. Flocks of lambs would be layered up around Melton on the day preceding the sale, or driven direct to the Church Meadow on the appointed day. Transportation from the sale, where speed was an important fac-

tor, was increasingly by rail and later by road.

Robert Bond, the long-established Ipswich auctioneers, were nominally in charge of organising the sale. However, much of the practical work, particularly in setting up, transporting lambs to and from Melton, and in overseeing the smooth running of the sale, was carried out by the Blosses. Fred Bloss (1878-1965) was, as one local put it, 'the power behind the throne'. He and his family had a high reputation within the farming fraternity. Fred was personally held in high esteem and trusted throughout the county and beyond. Melton Church meadow belonged to him. Buyers, both local and throughout East Anglia, would commission him to purchase for them and leave him to organise transport for them. Lambs would be 'exported' not only locally and to neighbouring counties but as far afield as Ireland. Security of payment for buyers was often given by him to Bond's. At its height in the inter-War years more than 10,000 lambs would change hands at Melton.

The annual lamb sale was very much a social and village event. Farmers met to discuss business and associated matters; the public houses with their extended hours of drinking by special licence and the village shops (in the broadest sense, not just retail outlets but builders, foundry, blacksmiths, wheelwrights etc.) were assured of a roaring trade for that day. Local children, particularly the boys, would play truant from school (Mr Bentham was always, and for long after his retirement, to be seen during the day at the Church Meadow in an attempt to spot local pupils and ex-pupils). As one old Meltonian put it "... *In my young days the whole village turned out; it was an occasion, an opportunity to meet distant family and friends.*" Just as at other events which involved work, business and excitement, there would always be a lot of bystanders - more bystanders than participants! The guaranteed excitement was centred on the actual sale but spread far beyond, beginning early in the morning and continuing until late afternoon.

At the end of the day the Blosses entertained at The Firs, their Melton home. This social part was very much a private affair and restricted to selected guests - always the same, all con-

**Mid-twentieth century pen and ink drawing of St. Andrew's Church from the Church Meadow – now St. Andrew's Place**

**Old byway leading to the Church Meadow and used by drovers in the nineteeth century to avoid the busy main roads**

nected with the sale, and all male. The format never varied: a substantial supper of roast beef, followed by trifles and a special 'tipsy cake'. Then the serious part of the evening commenced - playing Loo - which would end promptly at 11 p.m. with a tot of whisky and the departure of the guests.

*'A long but happy day.'*

**Melton Forge, 1994**

**Jack Blake (left) and Len Moore with restored traction engine, photographed in the mid-1970s**

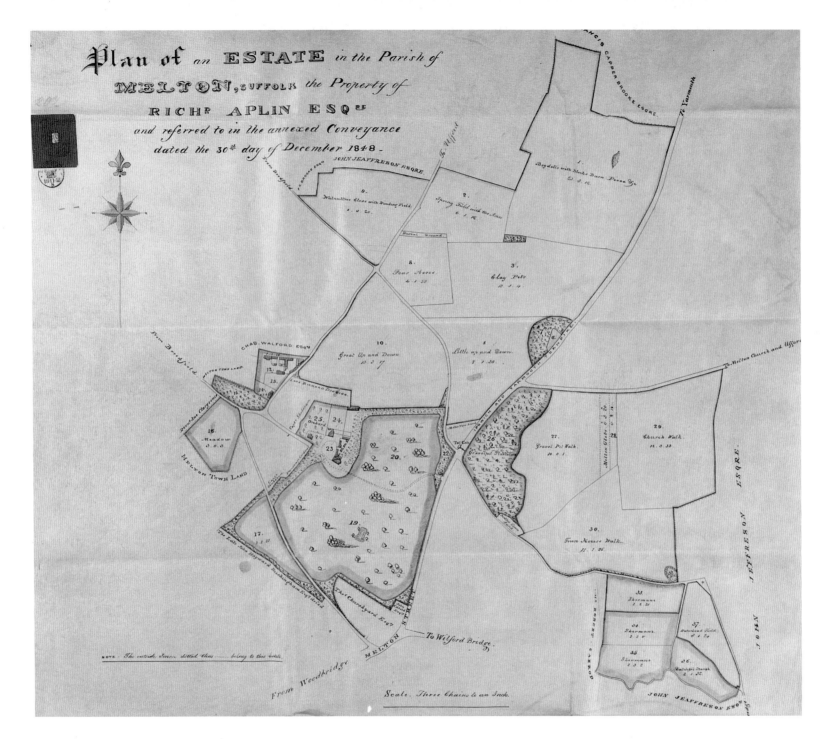

**1848 Map of Richard Alpin's Estate in the Parish of Melton**

**Close-up of Parish Church**

**View from Wilford Bridge**

**Looking northwards**

# A *brief history of the* Melton Poors Estate Charity

The history is scanty and at times appears disconnected owing to unavailability of official facts, but it appears that the Melton Charities were derived from several sources, which included:

1  *The Will of Richard Cook dated 12th July 1539*
2  *The Will of Robert Halifax dated 3rd July 1699*
3  *A gentleman named Histed.*

The aforesaid Wills left certain lands, cottages, etc., the income from which was to be applied

a  *for the benefit of the poor of the Parish of Melton*
b  *for the maintenance and beautifying of the Melton Church.*

The enclosures given by Halifax and Histed were over thirteen Acres and called The Charity Lands and the rents of these lands were used for repairs to the Church and the purchasing of coals for the poor. There were several other enclosures totalling over twenty seven acres belonging to the Church and called the Church Lands, the money from which went for repairs to the Church.

John Jenner later gave land known as Green Man Meadow (and later as Upper and Lower Jenners Dole) containing altogether 2 acres, 1 rood, 12 poles, which was used by the poor as Allotments.

In a deed of 23rd March 1811, the Trusts are stated to be as follows:

*"In trust and upon trust and confidence nevertheless, that the rents, issues and profits of the said hereditaments and premises shall be employed solely for the use and benefit of the said Town of Melton and for and towards the maintaining, supporting and beautifying the Parish Church of Melton aforesaid and all and every the ornaments and appurtenances thereunto, belonging to and for no other use, interest or purpose whatsoever."*

Previous to 1839 the general expenses of the Church Services were paid out of the Trust Funds. About that date new Trustees were appointed and up to 1858 such expenses were defrayed by Church Rates.

Since 1858 there has been no Church Rate and the Church expenses have been paid by the Trustees of the lands in question, which were called "The Church Lands".

For some years before 1840 the Rector and Churchwardens apparently received the rents and income from the Trust Estate and blended them in one account and expended the money partly in relief of the poor and partly in repairing the Church.

About this time the Trustees themselves collected the rents and made what they considered a proper division and application of the Trust Funds. Several questions, however, thereafter arose as to the expenditure of the funds and cases were in 1840, 1862 and 1870 submitted to Counsel with reference to the difficulties which had arisen.

Fortunately a Terrier of both the Church and Charity Lands was in existence in 1753 and several Terriers were subsequently prepared and are in existence. There is also an old Map of 1771 in which both the Church and Charity Lands are described.

The accumulated funds in the Lands of the Trustees were apportioned as accurately as possible between the two estates, i.e. £166-13-4 new Consols was placed to the credit of the Poors Estate and £450 new Consols to the credit of the Church Estate. The enclosures of lands were also apportioned accordingly.

There is also another Charity, that of James Alexander Burness founded by his Will of 20th November 1917 that upon his death (18th June 1920):

*"I bequeath the following legacies, all free of all duty, To the Trustees of the Poors Estate in Melton in the County of Suffolk, the sum of £1,000 2$\frac{1}{2}$% Consols upon trust to apply the income thereof in supplying bread and coal to the necessitous inhabitants of the Parish of Melton Forever."*

The endowment of this Charity is now represented by a sum of £1,000 2$\frac{1}{2}$% Consolidated Stock, held by the Official Trustees of Charitable Funds.

In 1897 the Trustees applied to the Charity Commissioners for, and on 29th June 1897, obtained an order making division of the real property between the Church Estate Charity and Poor Estate Charity. The Charity Commissioners further stated that the Trustees of the Poors' Estate Charity shall consist of the existing Trustees of the original Charity, other than the Churchwardens and that two persons to be appointed from time to time by the Melton Parish Council.

On 7th February 1973 the lands known as Upper and Lower Jenners Dole (Allotments) was sold by the Poors Estate and the money invested in C.O.I.F. Income Shares. It was also decided that from then onward the issue of bread and coal as a Christmas gift to the poor and aged parishioners should cease and a cash gift should take its place.

Following later discussions between the Charity Commission, the Parish Council and the Poors Estate Trustees, it was agreed that a new constitution be submitted and Trustees be appointed as follows:

1   *Three Trustees from Melton Parish Council*
    *(to serve for four years).*
2   *At least two non-Council Trustees*
    *(including Priest-in-Charge if possible).*
3   *One Clerk, including roll of Secretary and Treasurer.*
    *(To serve for three years).*

This was formalised and commenced on 12th October 1987 and continues to date.

The wording *"Melton Estate Trust"* is put on cards issued with the Christmas gift, as a means of avoiding embarrassment to those wishing to receive from a Poors Charity. Our official registered Charity is still known as the *"Melton Poors Estate Charity"*.

*Arthur A. Calder*
*Clerk & Secretary to the Melton Poors Estate Charity*

**Waterhead Lane - Almshouses built under the terms of Richard Cook's 1539 will, and demolished in the late 1940s**

# MELTON W. I.

*Programme for 1994*

**All monthly meetings are held in St Andrews Church Hall, Melton,
on a Tuesday at 7.30 pm. For further details, please contact the Secretary.**
## NEW MEMBERS ALWAYS WELCOME

| | | | |
|---|---|---|---|
| **January 25th** | Suffolk Rescue Service | **July 26th** | Walk around Ipswich |
| **February 22nd** | Aromatherapy | **August 23rd** | Samaritans |
| **March 22nd** | Museum of East Anglian Life | **September 27th** | Creative Embroidery |
| **April 26th** | Fans | **October 25th** | Dow Egberts |
| **May 24th** | Resolutions | **November 22nd** | Annual Meeting |
| **June 28th** | Environmental Health | **December 13th** | Christmas Social |

# Melton Women's Institute

**M**any of the organizations and clubs listed in the Melton Directory have been flourishing for many years and have received the support of the parish for several generations. For instance the need for improved sports facilities lead to the removal of the playing field to its present venue in the early post war period and over the years it has proved to be an ideal setting for a range of sports – including cycle speedways (in the early days), cricket, hockey and of course tennis and football. The Brownies, Guides and Scouts continue to attract and maintain support – albeit as with other Melton social groups from a wider catchment area often well outside the parish boundaries.

The Melton Women's Institute branch is one organization which in the 1980s seemed doomed to close – and which finally did. However now revitalised and with a much younger membership it now 'operates' as a go-ahead branch, offering a wide range of activities to an equally wide age range of members.

For over 60 years Melton WI met on the first Wednesday of every month, latterly at 2.30pm. The membership dwindled and eventually the Institute had to close.

In the autumn of 1991 a meeting was called by Suffolk East Federation of Women's Institutes for anyone interested in re-forming the Melton WI. There was found to be sufficient interest and in November of 1991 a committee was elected and subscriptions taken from 15 founder members. It was agreed that the women of the village could no longer freely attend daytime meetings due to work or child care commitments, therefore it was decided to meet on the 4th Tuesday of each month at 7.30pm, perhaps reflecting women's evolving role in society.

The founder members were drawn from a wide age range, with varying backgrounds and interests, all wishing to meet local people and make new friends.

Since then the membership has swelled and currently stands at 30 members. We have had many interesting meetings covering a variety of subjects including: Back from Beirut, Reflexology, Recycling, The History of Melton and Looking Good & Feeling Great.

We have also been on the number of outings including a visit to the Tolly Cobbold Brewery, a boat trip on the Deben and Christmas shopping trips every year by coach (which are much more fun with your friends).

At every May meeting we have to debate the National Resolutions of the WI on subjects of major importance such as Organ Donation, Patenting of Life Forms and Legal Aid, our decisions being carried forward to National Meetings. We always lighten this evening with a recipe swap and tasting of some delicacy. Such doings result in the production of our annual cookery book.

The Jam and Jerusalem image of the WI does not prevail in Melton. We are a friendly and approachable group and new members are always welcomed.

*Nicola Clarke - President*
*3, Fayrefield Road, Melton*
*Tel. 384861*

79   Melton Lodge, 1924

# Village Secrets & Mysteries

## Melton Rectories

Land was given to build the first Rectory in the twelfth century, its location being on rising ground between the present Hermitage and Melton Lodge. In 1872 James Packe bought the old Rectory to include the site in his estate. The house and buildings were by then in a 'somewhat neglected and derelict state' as recorded by the Rev. Christopher George Watson, Rector of Melton from 1814 - 1870, who had also been the stipendiary curate of Loudham Cum Pettistree and resided for the greater part of his incumbency in Woodbridge. Small wonder James Packe quickly demolished the former Rectory as Melton Lodge was being considerably enlarged and 'gentrified' at this time. In addition the old Rectory must have overlooked the Lodge.

Over the years sightings of a figure dressed in a long black cloak and wearing a flat hat have been reported by several people in this area. It is presumed that this is one of the old Rectors looking for his former house! A further mystery concerns the attractive Regency period cottage near the site of the old Rectory which pre-dates William Packe's enlargement of Melton Lodge. Also, interestingly, the cottage faces more or less due north looking upwards towards rising ground, having only very limited views to the south (which would be the natural aspect). This may well have formed part of the Rectory complex. Recently two large stone gargoyles dating from the twelfth or thirteenth century have been found in the area. To what building did they belong? Were they from an early castellated construction (which is how the original Rectory-house is described) or were they brought to the site from some distance? Certainly in the last century there was a vogue for creating romantic rockeries, grottoes and the like. And to support this theory, in the gardens of Melton Lodge are some Victorian composition stone figures which appear to be the work of Lockwood and Pulham, the 19th century Woodbridge based firm who specialised in cement manufacture, producing a range of ornamental buildings, figures, urns etc.

**Regency cottage near the site of the old Rectory**

**One of two stone gargoyles found near site of old Rectory**

## Margaret Catchpole's connections with Melton

Margaret Catchpole, the real-life heroine of Richard Cobbold's famous Victorian novel, passed through Melton on her way to Sudbourne following her dramatic escape from Ipswich Gaol on the night of March 25th 1800. While waiting for a smuggler's cutter to take her abroad to freedom, she was re-captured by Mr Ripshaw, the gaoler. On the return journey to Ipswich Mr Ripshaw and the Melton constable took dinner at the Horse and Groom. Local legend has it that Margaret was kept secretly overnight at the Horse and Groom because feeling in the area was running high in her favour and an attempt to free her was feared if she had been kept in Melton Gaol or had been escorted over Rushmere Heath during the hours of darkness. To substantiate this tale, Melton Gaol had, in fact, recently ceased to be used for housing prisoners on a regular basis. To this day a small upstairs room in the Horse and Groom, in which she is reputed to have stayed, is named after her.

It has long been rumoured within the Tampin and Daines families of Melton that they were related in some way to Margaret Catchpole. On November 6th 1861, William Tampin of Melton married Susan Catchpole of Bredfield at Melton Church. Their daughter Leah subsequently married Charles Daines. Susan Catchpole's great grandfather, Thomas, appears to have been the illegitimate son of Sarah Catchpole, who became Sarah Leader, or "Aunt Leader", mentioned by Margaret in her letters from Australia. Margaret was herself illegitimate and was brought up by Aunt Leader in Brandeston. Thomas was eight years older than Margaret and they probably grew up as brother and sister. It seems that this is one family legend with more than a grain of truth in it.

## Lay burial place in Melton

## Mausoleum For Sale - £100

*"At the bottom of a residence called The Retreat there stands a Summer house, of white brick, now locked and overgrown with creepers. Therein was buried, about 1878, a Mr Dean, described in White's Directory of 1868 as Stephen John Dean Esq of The Retreat, Melton.*

*His inscribed gravestone is said to form the floor of the Summer house."*

*From The East Anglian Miscellany, 1933.*

*"Brick-built mausoleum in the garden of The Retreat Melton to be sold by Messrs. Arnott and Calver, Woodbridge. The building, constructed of Suffolk white brick, measures twelve feet by ten feet with a curved roof; the floor has, inset, a stone slab with the inscription:*

*"Stephen James Dean, many years an Essex ship-owner born at Chelmsford in 1806 and died June 1871.*
*How beautiful this world, emerald gem*
*Shrined in all glorious sapphir lost, lost, lost,*
*Passed are the everlastingly closed gate of mortal life Behind them on the lap of mystery, dumb mute I darkly sit, To earth a blank, the earth a blank to me."*

*The author Richard Coeur de Lion. "An historical tragedy."*

*The mausoleum has been used as a Summer house.*
*Evening Star, 1st July 1966.*

It would appear that Mr. Dean had no faith in the Established Church and that there was animosity between him and the Melton Rector. As a man of some wealth and independent spirit he was determined not to rest in consecrated ground; thus he conceived the plan to be buried in his own land. Bilby Brothers, the village builders and undertakers, were commissioned to make his coffin and for some years this was kept at their yard opposite the New Church. However, eventually they insisted upon delivering the 'receptacle' to its owner; ironically Mr. Dean died soon after, and his wish to be buried in his Mausoleum was complied with.

The Mausoleum still stands, although somewhat decayed, in the garden at The Retreat, as a guardian over the mortal remains of Mr. Dean. There is no public right of way and no access to the Mausoleum.

# A Builder of Quality

A twentieth century Melton character of note was William Marjoram (1849-1935). In his earlier days he was a builder of some repute in the area, and examples of his craftsmanship remain, notably a somewhat austere and large residential dwelling of unusual design (10,12 & 14 Bredfield Road, Melton). More spectacular is Castle Cote next door where he and his wife Emma spent their declining years. The late Mrs Winifred Hayles gave her personal memories of her great uncle and aunt in a letter dated 1982:

"My great uncle was a striking figure with a snowy white beard and a full white head of hair. (A Melton artist Edmund Van Someren painted his portrait which was exhibited.) The old gentleman was somewhat eccentric and I think might have described himself as a British Israelite, having much interest in the two lost tribes of Israel."

The foregoing information is confirmed not only by the location of Van Someren's portrait of William Marjoram but also personal memories of older Meltonians. "He was obsessed with the Old Testament and would lecture anyone who was unable to escape." However, few locals knew of the folly secreted in his back garden.

In 1915 Woodbridge was subjected to a Zeppelin air-raid which caused not only loss of life and considerable damage but also fear amounting to panic among the local population. William Marjoram, with his knowledge of building, quickly realised the only way to provide safety for his family was by the construction of an air-raid shelter and he proceeded at great speed on this project which was completed early in 1917. As with his other work, his design showed not only originality but also the quality of the construction which must have involved considerable excavation and the use of tons of stone and cement. Considering that the 'construction' has stood for some eighty years any visitor* is immediately impressed with not only the workmanship but also its state of repair. Entering by a stone spiral stairway one descends to a circular stone chamber 9 feet in diameter and at an overall depth of 20 feet. However, the beau-

**Castle Cote, built by William Marjoram and his home for many years until his death in 1935**

* The shelter is on private property and is not open to the public.

tifully decorated walls which are covered with engraved texts and extracts from the Old Testament were, it is presumed, intended for meditation during the possibly long hours spent underground. William Marjoram clearly intended his work to be something of a personal memorial - strategically placed at the entrance the following quotation is significant:

*'The writer of these lines and the texts of scripture in and about this dug-out respectfully ask that this may be protected from obliteration or damage, remembering always that all scripture is given by the inspiration of God, and pray that all who protect them may be blessed bodily and spiritually ... '*

Signed W.M.

**William Marjoram in old age
an oil painting by Edward van Someren, c1930**

# A *village secret (which did not materialise)*

January 11th, 1951: Sir Roland Burk as County Councillor addressed the Parish Council. He emphasised at the outset that the Council must treat in the strictest confidence that he had been informed by Mr Reed of the Rural Community Council that in all probability the Duke of Edinburgh would be paying an official visit to Ipswich and district in the autumn. It was felt that it would be fitting that the Duke, as President of the National Playing Fields Association, should officially open a new recreation ground in East Suffolk. As Melton was in the process of moving their playing field from the Garrard Memorial Playing Field in Dock Lane to the present location in Melton Road, the village was considered a most favourable venue .

After some discussion (by the Council) it was agreed that such an opening would be a very desirable event, even though the ground would not be ready for full use until 1952. It was further agreed that the Parish Council Chairman and Vice-Chairman should see Mr Reed and put the full position before him.

Not surprisingly the spring and summer of 1951 witnessed rapid progress in the development of the new playing field. Alas, for reasons no longer clear the proposed visit did not materialise. However, Melton's new playing field was fully operational in record time and remains a focal point of village life.

**Sir Roland and Lady Burk**
**photographed at Melton Mead on their Golden Wedding**

# Thursday night

*"We always got to bed in good time on Thursdays and it was a night when we kids knew that something was afoot. We often heard a vehicle making its way down our lane, stopping and starting, doors and gates being opened and closed and muffled voices sounding on occasions. Father came home in good time from the pub on Thursdays. My older sisters (with whom I shared a double feather bed) would scare me stiff with tales of bogeymen (or Old Diddler★) coming to get me. No wonder my mother dreaded the recurring nightmares I suffered from on Thursdays and gave my sisters strict instructions not to torment me. In truth I now believe we all were petrified and slept lightly until the weekly visitation had passed."*

Throughout Melton there used to be an air of growing expectancy on Thursday evenings. Special preparations were required and understood by all those involved in the weekly ritual. Windows were tightly closed both in summer and winter; back gates were left unlocked, and obstacles such as bins, buckets, watering cans, and – most important – linen lines, were put aside. For those homes having no rear access the front door would remain unbolted and newspapers carefully laid from front to back door. The furniture would be pushed back to allow a safe passage out to the small building usually situated in the back yard, being a lean-to from the main dwelling.

One particularly conscientious and houseproud lady always insisted upon waiting up to 'welcome' and supervise the operation carried out by her weekly visitors. According to her daughter, Mother spent upwards of an hour in careful preparation. Furniture was not only moved to make as wide a passage as possible from front to back door, but every piece was carefully covered in freshly laundered old sheets (dust sheets). The floor was completely covered with overlapping back copies of the East Anglian Daily Times (then in broadsheet). Jeyes Fluid had been liberally dispensed down the kitchen sink and the outside drains; in addition the good lady insisted upon having a jug of strong disinfectant ready for any emergency. During winter months, when fires heated her front parlour, dried lavender was kept ready to be sprinkled on the hearth shovel and over the dying embers upon

the visitors' arrival.

The wait could be long – delays en route were not uncommon  conversations with any who cared to linger were encouraged by the team (if not the recipients). Added to this, the team were renowned both for their care and independence as they worked largely unsupervised by either employers or clients. Mrs X continued to sit regally in her fireside chair until she heard sounds of their approach.  At the precise and always the right moment (according to her daughter), Mother would open her front door and usher the visitor in.  No greeting usually ensued. Much to the family's embarrassment the good lady insisted upon supervising the whole operation in the most minute detail. A whole series of commands and requests would accompany the task being carried out: "Do be careful – My yard is slippery/icy tonight – I've left my geraniums to enjoy the gentle rain - Do mind your feet" and so on! In exasperation on one occasion 'Old Winkle', the gang leader, suggested to Mrs X that she might like to join the team for a ride down Melton Street. The offer was not accepted and conversation was severely curtailed for many weeks!

After they had left an equally protracted series of rituals were carried out: newspapers either to be binned for Monday's refuse collection or to be made into firelighters (those furthest from any possible contamination would be folded for use next week). Dust sheets were meticulously examined before being folded and put away for the next Thursday night (the lady had a careful system of rotating the washing of dust sheets to ensure that each was boiled every three to four weeks). Next, all the downstairs floors were swept; in addition the kitchen and tiny scullery brick floors were wiped over with the floor cloth liberally sprinkled from the jug of disinfectant (these floors were the traditional white Suffolk floor pannetts and would be scrubbed every Monday with hot soapy water from the copper after the weekly wash had been boiled). A final dusting and inspection throughout the ground floor of the cottage was completed. Lastly, the front and back doors were bolted and the matriarch would ascend to join her spouse. However, there would often be only four to five hours

★ A local character who will feature in later books on the district.

before she arose at 6.15 a.m. to re-inspect the interior of her home and carefully sweep the backyard – scrubbing the 'little house' in the yard (politely known in the family as the 'reading room') – scrubbed twice weekly Monday and Friday a.m.

As Christmas approached, danger and the chance of unpleasant accidents increased. Alcohol was the chief culprit. In order to steady nerves and share the festive spirit the team would more frequently have "a pint or two" (or more!) before they left their Woodbridge base. Appreciative clients, particularly those who relied upon a careful passage through their homes, were more inclined to leave tots of spirit or small bottles of beer (this could be drunk by a confident handler while negotiating and lifting a heavy utensil with the other arm). After copious liquid refreshment, and as their journey through Melton neared its completion, the team could well become less steady on their legs; co-ordination between lifting and carrying and avoiding obstacles deteriorated. On one disastrous night Miss X forgot to remove her linen line and this resulted in not only the operator losing his footing but also the contents of the utensil being spread across the backyard!

A trick regularly carried out when the vehicle was horse drawn would be to move it further down the road. At best this necessitated a longer walk for the operators. At worst accidents were known to occur.

One summer night a motorcycle ran straight into the stationary vehicle at the bottom of Melton Hill. At least two miracles were recorded: neither rider nor pillion was seriously hurt, but the latter was catapulted straight into the open container and had to be helped out (fortunately this was at the early stages of the night's work when it was only partially full). Not only did the pillion rider have to endure a cold bucket shower before being allowed admittance to his home by an irate and unsympathetic wife, but evidence of the accident (paper and debris) was thrown up into the overhanging trees, much to the concern, not to say amusement, of the local adults and children.

Ideas of hygiene have changed. The cart always stopped at least once so that the men could have a break from their work and eat their packed 'bait'. ('Bait' feeding both men and working horses.) One of the hazards especially if liquid refreshment had been taken either before or en route was the danger of dropping one's wrapped sandwiches in the open cart, which, it has been claimed, necessitated 'fishing' to retrieve them.

The wife of one such council worker was always impressed by her husband's beautiful clean hands, which might be explained by the bleaching qualities attributed to one of the commodities he would often meet in his work.

The 'honey-cart' in the post-war period became an increasing anachronism as all new houses had full sanitary planning and older properties were modernised. The weekly call, far from being a status symbol, became identified with social and economic degradation. It finally ceased in the mid nineteen-sixties when Melton was linked to the main sewerage system.

*From the Parish Council records*

9.5.1946: Notice received from the contractor for the removal of night-soil that he is giving up the work the week after 11th May. After the matter had been fully discussed one possible remedy was to increase the weekly fee from £5 to £6.

27.6.1946: Night-soil. Note received through the offices of the Deben Rural District Council that the contractor responsible was raising his price from £5 a week to "about £6" and consequently the matter was "by no means settled". At this juncture the Chairman read a letter from Mr. Firman (Parish Councillor) who apologised for not mentioning earlier that two 'pit closets' normally emptied every 3 months had now been left for over 9 months.

The Council wrote a further letter to the D.R.D.C. expressing their anxiety but emphasising that a contractor should not be lost on account of expense, unless the price being asked was "really excessive". Not surprisingly £7 was later in 1946 agreed as a satisfactory weekly fee.

*It is worthy of note that the average weekly wage was still under £2 for unskilled work, and that this particular task was only carried out once a week (of course a vehicle had to be supplied and maintained and three men were usually involved in the teamwork). This may be indicative of how unpleasant to perform this particular public service was rated.*

## Methods of sanitation in common use - pre-1960

1. Those households relying upon the weekly Thursday night collection.

2. 'Bucket and chuck it' i.e. emptying the nightsoil oneself (or often by a tame employee or 'friend'). Don Friar records that this method applied to his father's business and house waste until well into the post-War period. The 'soil' was added to the garden and, it was claimed privately, helped to account for the excellent produce grown and sold in their shop.

3. Collection of night-soil, which had accumulated in a pit, often brick lined, behind the outside 'bumby'. This task would either be the responsibility of the householder or by special arrangement with the 'honey-cart brigade' (this work was normally carried out either on the preceding or following night (after Thursday) much to the consternation of neighbours and the embarrassment of those responsible).

The 1945 Parish Council minutes record that one household normally receiving this service quarterly had been waiting for over 9 months!

4. The water closet (W.C.) was the height of social 'arrival'. Until the inter-War years only the big houses and those occupied by the 'upper crust' had inside water sanitation. Earlier, sand and ash lavatories had been in use in many houses. However, the mechanics for depositing the sand or ash were often not reliable; Melton Hall for instance in the early part of the twentieth century had such a lavatory, which continually needed repair and improvisation by local businessmen. (The Bilby Day Book confirms this.)

As the twentieth century progressed and a mains sewerage system became more readily available, an increasing number of homes had W.C.s fitted, often utilising the former outside lavatory building. Each house or group of houses (if owned by one landlord) had its own cesspit or 'deadwell', which would periodically be emptied by W.R.D.C. (Woodbridge Rural District Council). In the case of Robert Blake's former home, the cesspit was never emptied but a nearby Bramley apple tree produced record, and delicious, crops for a number of years.

*A few colloquialisms for the outside lavatory:*
*'Privvy', 'Next-door', 'Bumby', 'Closet', 'Throne', 'House of correction', the 'Little house', the 'Dunny'.*

### A Saturday job

For many school children, Saturday morning was the time they were expected to earn their weekly pocket money. Boys and girls who were of a 'responsible age' would do shopping and errands for family, neighbours and friends. Gardening was the particular province for older boys and housework for teenage girls (many of whom would later find themselves 'in service', so this was a means of informal training). Younger children were often employed cutting old newspaper squares – approximately 4"x4" – for use in the 'privy' by the whole family for the forthcoming week. The squares, threaded on string, would be suspended from a nail.

89    Old Gaol, with buttress adjacent to Friar's Shop, c1920

**St. Audry's**

**Centre of the Village**

**From the river**

# Melton Horrors

For over eight centuries Melton Gaol stood in the centre of the village casting its shadow over the whole area. It was here that the court sessions were held and justice administered until 1575 when Thomas Seckford built the Shire Hall in Woodbridge and moved the Court there.

Prisoners, both infamous but in most instances petty criminals, were brought to Melton for sentencing. Punishment ranged from fines, public flogging, time spent in the stocks, incarceration or, more rarely, the death sentence. There were two local gallows sites, one on the hill beyond Wilford Bridge, the other on Mount Misery situated on the north west side of the village. However, if there was any likelihood of riot or rescue attempt being made the sentence would be carried out within the gaol complex, in which case a black flag would be flown from the end of the building.

**Thomas Churchyard watercolour of gypsy encampment below Gallows Hill**

The loss of status for Melton when the court was moved to Woodbridge must have been considerable and was not compensated for by the prison continuing in use for a further two centuries. The original court room, situated on the first floor, would have been handsome, an impression confirmed by later illustrations showing fine panelling with ornate carvings. When Dutch prisoners were held here after the battle of Sole Bay in 1665, they left behind carvings of ships and windmills reminiscent of home, which were still intact at the time of demolition in the early 1960s.

The location of a witchpit and Witchpit Farm near the present A12 on the periphery of the village recalls the practice of 'dunking' in water poor old women, strapped in a chair, to establish their innocence or guilt. The women were probably harmless, dealing in potions, spells and cures, but considered evil in superstitious times.

Punishment carried out in public had a dual function: justice could be seen to be administered, and was intended to be a deterrent for any would-be offenders. However, it was much more

**A carving by a Dutch prisoner in Melton Gaol after the Battle of Sole Bay**

than this, as it provided a spectacle enjoyed by the community, and offered a possible break in the monotony of contemporary life. Melton as an important route and trading centre provided an ideal venue for such events.

**Inside the Old Gaol, first floor chamber**

**Canon Wilkinson with the grizzly relic of Cromwell**

The late Canon H.R. Wilkinson of Melton Grove kept the mummified head of Oliver Cromwell in his house. The relic was shown to discerning visitors, including honoured Melton Scouts and choirboys during my youth; unfortunately (or fortunately) I personally never saw either the box in which it was kept or its grizzly contents.

Arthur Mee, in his famous 'King's England' series, for Suffolk writes:

*"It is an almost incredible spectacle with hair still clinging to it, with teeth still intact, with the forehead we are familiar with (even with the marks of the warts), and we are indebted to Canon Wilkinson for allowing us to see this astonishing relic of our greatest man of action".*

The embalmed head came into the safekeeping of the Wilkinson family early in the nineteenth century and became a family heirloom. After the death of Canon Wilkinson in 1957, his son, Dr. Horace Wilkinson, presented it to Sidney Sussex College, Cambridge, and it was later buried in secrecy within the precincts of the college.

Many myths and mysteries have been handed down from the past, but with only limited research, grounds for their authenticity cannot always be confirmed. Orford had its 'mermaid', Melton had its legendary 'shuck'. The following story has many local variations but essentially dates back to the mid-nineteenth century (which is late for such legends to originate) and centres on the Horse and Groom and the Toll Gate. Henry Fisher was the current landlord and his son's account was given to V.B. Redstone the well known local historian some 30-40 years later (at around the turn of the century):

*"In the days of the Toll Gates on a very dark night Goodman Kemp of Woodbridge entered the Inn in a hurried and frightened manner, and asked for the loan of a gun to shoot a 'shock' or 'shuck', which hung upon the Toll Bar Gates".*

The 'shuck' was a thing with a donkey's head and a smooth velvet hide. Kemp always maintained that he had attempted to grab the creature and take it to the Inn in order to examine it in a good light and also authenticate his story. However, it bit him "and vanished"; but "Kemp bore the marks of the 'shock's'/'shuck's' bite upon his thumb to his dying day". Not surprising that more than a century later tales of horrific creatures being seen in local woodland are commonplace.

In more recent times, the horrific dangers from local quicksands have been recorded. 'Bull's Hole' was the site where an unfortunate animal met its death.

93  Coronation procession through Melton Street, June 2nd, 1953

# Celebrations

## Queen Victoria's Golden Jubilee, 1887

All the necessary preparations for the due and loyal celebration of this auspicious event were made by a committee appointed at a General Meeting of the parishioners which included the Rector, Churchwardens, and Messrs. W. Bilby, F. Page, W. Scarff, F. Bloss and A. Skoulding.

Several triumphal arches were placed across the street, and garlands and flags hung from private houses. One arch was placed over the school gate, and all looked very gay.

The celebration commenced on Tuesday with a Thanksgiving service in the Church, and Hymn 379 (Now Thank We all our God) was sung as a processional. A short address was given by the Rector★, and the National Anthem was sung.

At 1 o'clock a dinner was given in the National School to about 250 men and women. The meal consisted of 'the good old English fare', and arrangements for its preparation were made by Mr. Bilby, ably assisted by his two sons, the room and tables being most tastefully decorated by the ladies of the Parish. After dinner, pipe and tobacco were provided. The only toast proposed was "The Health of her most gracious Majesty", which was most heartily and loyally responded to with "three times three". After singing the National Anthem the party adjourned to a suitable field, lent by Mr. Wood, where arrangements had been made for rural sports by the Messrs. Bilby (W., John and T.), H. Harris, W. Scarff and A. Tricker. There were a large number of entries for each of the 14 events; the competition was keen and caused much excitement and amusement.

While the sports were going on, the schoolroom was being arranged for a substantial Tea, which was thoroughly enjoyed by about 250 children and women who were prevented from being present at the dinner. Those persons who were too old, infirm, or too ill to come out, had their meal sent to their homes.

The Finale was a bonfire in Mr. Wood's field. All worked hard to make the Celebrations a success.

*From a contemporary Report.*

**Scarf heralding Queen Victoria's Golden Jubilee in 1887, worn as a neckerchief by Jack Blake for many years**

★ A villager attending this service notes that Rector spoke of the personal character and qualities of the Queen and the Imperial achievements during her reign; in addition he mentions that the 'Sermon' took a little less than one hour to deliver (a contemporary 'short' address!).

## The Melton Lights, 1897*

O, to sing in melting strains
A song of new delights!
Sound it o'er Leeks hills and plains
The joyful news of Melton Lights.

Like twinkling stars they shine
All down the Melton Road
Sunday night they looked so fine
As there the people strode.

Generations long had stumbled
Jostled on in blackest night,
Patient souls oft times grumbled
And deeply sighed for light.

Yet when the scheme was mooted,
Some thought would just explode
Or like a straw be floated
To leave in darkness Melton Road.

But on came the merry June,
Melton made a grand display
With every melting heart in tune
On the glorious 22nd day.

Twice the multitude was fed
With excellent ample fare
In sports and music the day soon sped,
Some felt all had ended there.

But ere that good Committee rose
They sent the edict all around Lo!
before the year shall close
Light much more shall abound.

So, enlightened Melton leads the way
And sheds a glory on our path,
The famous Road where courters stray
And sweet maidens skip and laugh.

Now Melton is astonished quite
And Woodbridge all stand gazing,
See our neighbours in another light
Oh dear, Oh dear, 'tis so amazing.

Fair Melton, thou hast done well
To bid our darkness flee,
Thy future sons shall tell
How you marked Diamond Jubilee!

*Queen Victoria's Diamond Jubilee*

*by T.D. Symonds*

*   See Melton street lighting p.104

# V. E. Day

Thanksgiving Service at Church; children's sports on the following day for all parish children attending the village school. The Parish Council made a grant of £20* towards expenses - which would include CASH Prizes, simple refreshments and soft drinks, plus oranges if possible. Mr. Keeble (the headmaster) had complete responsibility for organising the event.

**"Welcome Home" Supper
after the Second World War
May 11th, 1946**

\* £12.7.11. expended, therefore £7.12.1. refunded
and paid into bank!

*Elizabeth R.*
1953

# MELTON
## Tuesday, June 2nd, 1953

*Programme of Festivities*

In Celebration of the

# CORONATION

of

## Her Majesty
## Queen Elizabeth II.

MUSIC will be provided during the afternoon and evening.

SOUVENIR MUGS will be presented to all children not attending school.

ON SUNDAY, May 31st there will be a special Service in St. Andrews Church, Melton, at 11.00 a.m., in preparation for the Coronation.

PRIZES will be awarded for the Best Decorated frontages of houses, and houses with gardens.

Programme of Sports is attached to this Souvenir Programme.

## Programme

| | |
|---|---|
| 8.00 a.m. | HOLY COMMUNION |
| 9.15 a.m. | SHORT SERVICE in St. Andrew's Church. |
| 2.00 p.m. | CARNIVAL PROCESSION (Commencing at the Church Meadow) |
| 2.30 p.m. | UNVEILING OF PLAQUE FOR CORONATION OAK |
| | SPORTS (Children & Adults) at Playing field |
| 4.30 p.m. | CHILDREN'S TEA (In the Old Chapel, MELTON) |
| 5.30 p.m. | CONTINUATION of Sports |
| 7.30 p.m. | CONCERT for Old People (in Parish Room) |
| 10.30 p.m. | TORCHLIGHT PROCESSION (Commencing at the Church Meadow) |
| 11.00 p.m. | LIGHTING OF BONFIRE and FIREWORKS |

God Save the Queen

99    **Looking up The Street early this century – note the absence of pavements**

# Vignettes

## Pig-keeping in Melton

Complaints concerning objectionable smells originating in Melton street were circulating during the winter months of 1945/46. From a letter received by the Parish Council in 1946 it appeared that the smells were coming from unoccupied, condemned cottages in the centre of the village in near proximity to the butcher's shop. It is salient that no mention is made in the Council minutes of either the exact location of the property, or its owner. It is clear that the Parish Council were showing both discretion and tolerance (and perhaps some sympathy for the owner) as it later became evident that these "village smells" were caused by pigs being kept in the said properties.

27.6.1946: It was reported that "following an inspection of the condemned cottages in Melton Street the pigs being kept there had been moved further from the road" (Parish Council records).

Obviously the pigs were still being kept but restricted to the back kitchens and outhouses, which is indicative of a united effort to bring compromise in what could have been a delicate situation. However, it is worthy of note that rationing was still being applied and the home production of pork and bacon was considered to be in the national interest.

**Looking south, towards the harness-maker, blacksmiths and foundry**

## Extracts from Churchwarden's Book, 1759-1810
## some Church expenses

| Year | Description | £ | s | d |
|---|---|---|---|---|
| 1770 | Thatching Church Stake (Stable)* | £2 | 3 | 6 |
| 1771 | For Thatching the Stable at ye Church | | 9 | 9 |
| 1772 | Mending the Window in the Church Steeple | | | 5 |
| 1775 | Mending the Leads of the Church | | 18 | 10 |
| 1775 | Paid the Thatcher's Bill | | 10 | 2½ |
| 1786 | Repairing & Whitewashing the Church | 2 | 19 | 11 |
| | 2 Women for Cleaning | | 2 | 6 |
| | Beer for Plasterers & Women | | 2 | 0 |
| 1793 | Erecting Partition in Steeple | 1 | 10 | 0 |
| 1794 | Painting Communion Rail | 1 | 14 | 2 |
| | Repairing & Whitewashing | 1 | 4 | 8 |
| 1795 | Repairs & Materials | 2 | 17 | 1 |
| 1796 | Materials for Church Stable | 1 | 6 | 7½ |
| | Church Window Leading | 5 | 6 | 3 |
| 1797 | Repairs Outside & Inside | 1 | 7 | 10 |
| | Women Cleaners & Beer | | 8 | 2 |
| 1799 | Repairs | 1 | 5 | 2 |
| | Materials for Pulpit Desk, Cushion etc. | 3 | 3 | 0 |
| 1801 | Fringe, 4 large Tassels, Green Baize, | | | |
| | Brass Nails, etc. | 6 | 19 | 0 |
| 1802 | Repairs | 3 | 3 | 9 |
| 1804 | New Windows | 5 | 10 | 0 |
| 1805 | Straw & Carting | 6 | 3 | 0 |
| | For Thatching Church Stable | 2 | 3 | 6 |
| 1806 | Repairs & Cleaning | 2 | 0 | 10 |

* Note: Straw for thatching a cottage cost £1  4  0

# Peace

Such Peace - I think the Earth stood still and listened.
Green fields swept far to meet the dim unknown.
The end of all was sky – grass tree and river,
All drew towards it – seemed to touch, and pass.
So vast, my soul drank of that cup of silence.
A tender wind stirred in the moving grass
Lulled was the storm, and in the calm that followed,
The stillness and the silence held a voice.

*Violet Churchman*
*(1902-1993)*

**Still life by Dorothy Churchman (1897 - 1967)**

## Footprints

I walked the shore in the early morn,
And watched in wonder a day reborn.
I saw the surge of the rolling tide
With white horses on the waves that ride.

I searched my mind an answer to find,
When I turned and looked way back behind
And saw my imprints in the sand so clear
So I stopped and thought in sudden fear.

Just like life as we go on our way,
We leave behind imprints of things we do and say,
So that others that follow our footsteps will know
The way may be clear like the footprints below.

*Taken from:*

*"Suffolk Gems"*

*A collection of poems by Rosie Caulfield who has been a Melton
resident for more than 50 years*

**Mr & Mrs Caulfield's 'Golden Wedding'**

## Melton Street Lighting

*1897:*

The village was able to celebrate not only Queen Victoria's Jubilee but also the installation of gas street lighting. This was some months ahead of Woodbridge and gave great kudos to Melton, "the poorer but respectable relative" (contemporary Meltonian's assessment).

*1939-45:*

For reasons of national security many electric street lights were reduced in wattage.

*1942:*

Two newly installed electric light standards near Wilford Bridge were provided with 15 watt bulbs owing to the vulnerability and strategic importance of this Deben crossing.

*1946:*

(After V E Day celebrations) The Parish Council minutes record the cost of electricity per street light:

£2  8s.6d.  40 watt bulb per lamp

£2.12s.0d.  60 watt bulb per lamp

£2.18s.6d. 100 watt bulb per lamp.

"It was unanimously agreed to retain 40 watt bulbs."

## The Sparrow War

A recurring item of expense as recorded in Melton Church Warden's Book 1759-1837. One farthing was paid for each bird killed. 1772 5/7$\frac{1}{2}$d paid for 22$\frac{1}{2}$ dozen (and for breaking 201 eggs); later the killing of 28 dozen and the highest recorded figure being 52 dozen in one year. This indicates the continual battle to keep sparrows from damaging thatched roofs, including domestic and agricultural buildings and thatched stacks.

## National Savings Thanksgivings

*Oct 8-13, 1945*

Melton target fixed at £4,500. In fact £4,702.11.3 raised – no mean achievement after six difficult and costly years at war.

## 1977

Supper and Entertainment for all Pensioners in Melton held on August 20th in the Parish Room, at 6.00 for 6.30 pm. The Deben players provided the entertainment and the evening finished at 9.30 pm. Approximately 180 OAPs attended.

# Something about Melton and Melton Folks

*Written by a local Poet circa 1870*

1  They've two Churches and a Chapel, an Asylum and a Hall,
2  The Remnants of a prison, a River, Dock and Wall;
3  A Foundry, and a Carpentry, a place to build wind mills,
4  Two very honest Lawyers, so they never tax their bills.
5  They've a Wind Mill and a Water Mill, two Toll-bars and four Inns,
6  A Railway Station, Hamlet, and a Merchant Store with bins
7  Well filled with corn and cake and coals; a Malting they've also,
8  Three Justices, one ditto Clerk, a Colonel, Major too.
9  There are three of Seckford's Trustees, who also here reside,
10 Whose duty 'tis for poor old men and women to provide:
11 To see that every Almsman receives his proper dole,
12 And also every boy that's whacked at Seckford Grammar School.
13 They've two Bakers and a Butcher, all living in one street,
14 A sign to all that Bread is there more plentiful than Meat;
15 They've only one good Grocer's Shop, that's worthy of beholding;
16 Kept by a very quiet man, who always will be Skouldlng.
17 Their Foundry finds employment for youth and men of age,
18 And moulders, fitters, casters all, are governed by a Page,
19 His partner is a gentleman, possessing virtue sterling,
20 He is a jolly Bachelor, and always will be Girling.
21 There's Bilby builds them houses, and Collins builds them mills,
22 And as they have no Druggist they to Woodbridge send for pills;
23 But there's another Builder whose name I'd almost passed,
24 Be sure whatever work he does, it's always sure to Last.
25 Of poor folks they've of course their share, of gentlemen a Pack,

26 An average lot of wise men, and for mad men never lack,
27 Their Church clerk is a Chaplin, and a Shoeing-smith is he,
28 Their Curate also is a Smith, although no smith he be.
29 In Mechanics Last and Collins outshine Archimedes,
30 For they removed a Chapel whole, twelve feet, with perfect ease.
31 When Winter stern brought sleet and rain how oft 'twas wished they'd search,
32 For some expedient whereby they could remove the Church.
33 But now they've got a nice new Church, which thrice a day is filled,
34 Where Stidolph plays the organ, and gospel truth's instilled
35 By preacher into hearers, whether Woodbridge folks or no,
36 For lots of Woodbridge people to Melton Church do go.
37 But whether they are better than those who do not roam,
38 I cannot say, but Melton folks oft wish they'd stop at home,
39 Their company is very good, but better far their room.

*Extract from G. Booth's Almanack for 1914*

# Returning to Roots

"I spent my formative years in Melton. Attending the old school in the Street immediately brought me into contact with a cross-section of the community and I soon settled into the contemporary scene. Melton was then very much a traditional village with the church, school, Friar's shop, the Post Office, Bilby's the butchers, Max Skoulding in his paper shop and the blacksmith's in Station Road.

Unsophisticated sources of entertainment and pleasure for us children were largely supplied near to home, whether on the river, in the woods, on the recreation ground or, more organised, in the village scout and guide groups. Life had a seasonal pattern. In spring and summer we spent much time out of doors, playing with friends and neighbours and being free to wander where houses now stand. Particular memories are of spending hours on St. Andrew's Meadow after the Lamb Sale. We would crawl through a barrage of hurdles (no doubt covered with sheep droppings); later the grass was so rich and lush we would tunnel through it and hide from other children and unsuspecting adults. Near Bull's Hole Marsh, which was reputed to be full of quicksands, we had special dens where again we would hide from the big and, perhaps at times, alien world. Food eaten with our gang away from outsiders was one of the many happy rituals which occupied (as I remember) hot and sunny summer days. We collected tadpoles and other 'livestock' from streams and pools and delighted in taking them home in jamjars – some to be presented with great pride to our class Nature Table.

From June onwards right up to the end of the summer holidays Melton children were to be found 'swimming' near Hackney; it is only in later years that I appreciate the potential dangers, as few of us were competent swimmers and strong currents were a constant threat. Added to this, much raw sewage fed straight into the Deben. I well remember on one occasion having to walk back from Sutton 'beach' owing to the rising tide, which prevented us from swimming back to the Melton side. Speedway (that is cycle speedway) was another great interest during the summer months. We spent many happy long evenings first at Orford's farm (Potash Farm, in Doe's Alley), where Mr Orford

allowed us to construct a cinder track, and later on the more permanent track on the playing fields. My parents had certain reservations concerning my involvement in these activities but these were never clarified, nor was I formally stopped from attending. Scrumping apples was another annual event – McAndrews' orchards (at Bury Hill), despite threatening barbed wire, was a lucrative source.

As the days became shorter and the nights longer we met our friends often at pre-arranged spots within the village – one favourite being the fish and chip shop, where we pooled our pennies and shared bags of chips. One particular dare was to eat them within the sanctuary of St. Andrew's Church. Mr. Skoulding should have locked up at dusk, but either he went later or sometimes forgot – certainly we found access on many occasions and ate our feasts while playing games within its darkened confines. One or two friends took their dogs with them to bolster group confidence, which also added to the excitement!

Later I attended schools outside Melton, but my base was always here and my earliest friends and links continued through adolescence. However, I remained and still feel somewhat detached, as if one foot is here and another elsewhere.

From the mid-sixties to the eighties I moved away, marrying, having a family and establishing completely independent – another way or ways of life. I seemed to 'keep a foot in both camps', here and there. We regularly visited and stayed with family and friends in the village and neighbourhood. In retrospect perhaps I saw life in Melton increasingly through rose-coloured spectacles. I was aware of village changes during these years but I failed to register the insidious developments – more houses, more transport passing through and more people. Increasingly I thought of Melton as a safe place for children to grow up, contrasting and comparing our lifestyle with my own childhood and adolescence.

The most momentous decision was to return as residents of Melton. We had, I thought, considered all aspects of our move and felt quite confident that as a nuclear family unit with extended family and friends for support we could not only survive but would flourish living in Melton. The benefits from developments in the neighbourhood all seemed to be pluses – educational and recreational facilities for our children and increased employment prospects for us. New housing estates immediately offered potential for purchasing and giving a choice of home within the parish boundaries. In many respects these aspects were attained and in addition it quickly became apparent that many of the restrictive social structures of my youth had passed away. Village life in the mid-eighties was far more open than that of the nineteen-fifties or sixties. Melton was never – at least in my time – a beautiful village, but strategically placed, giving easy access to both the country and neighbouring towns and cities. We could all, as a family, contribute to local life, but also enjoy the benefits from mobility and good transport communications. We learnt, or re-learnt, to live a rich and varied life. My children became even more self-reliant and able to entertain themselves, whether on the river, riding, or at town discos and the like. The educational provisions we found to be as good as our expectations, and together with easy reach to London and beyond, we could bridge the geographical gap between our old and our present lifestyle.

The old insular way of life did not inhibit or perhaps restrict either myself (as formerly) and certainly not my children. There was on the other hand a feeling for me during those early months that I had only been away for a few days and not some twenty years. It was as if living in a time warp. Some situations and relationships within the community seemed almost not to have changed or developed despite a whole generation having grown up, albeit with the same prevailing pattern of expectation and behaviour, so that in some instances one could clearly anticipate responses. The difference, I now appreciate, was that I had changed beyond all recognition, being more worldly wise and self assured; in addition we as a nuclear family were more confident than some locals. I still wonder if we made the right decision. We could, I suspect, have settled into a similar environment which would have saved much soul-searching, particularly for me, and on-going inquests from my children and extended family as to

why we returned. I do think that it is natural to go back mentally if not physically to one's roots. We have all made conscious efforts to be accepted and to settle into the present Melton way of life (whatever that may mean). I feel a sense of satisfaction to be able to relate to family and friends living within the parish. As a close friend recently put it, "we seem to be in the village but not necessarily of it"."

*The anonymity of this contributor is respected by the author.*

# Survey of Melton Parishoners

As an essential part of research into the history and present day life of Melton we aimed to contact each household in the village by questionnaire, which asked briefly what they felt about Melton and any information they had that would be of interest (questionnaire copy Appendix 2).

Seventy-three questionnaires were returned representing 187 people. The majority of questionnaires, 59, were received from families of two, three or four people, eleven people lived alone and three families lived with five or more people. There were 32 children, 77 women and 79 men. Six people were over 80 years of age.

The length of time that the families had lived in Melton ranged from 78 years to one year. The average length was sixteen and a half years. More than half the families had lived for over nine years in the village.

Many of the families would like to see some changes in Melton. Three families would like to see less traffic travelling through the village, but another two would like to see more shops. Other suggestions relating to traffic were:

- a crossing at Wilford Bridge
- a roundabout, not traffic lights, at the bottom of Woods Lane
- better car-parking facilities for the school
- a lower speed limit and provision for cyclists
- better access for traffic at Turnpike Lane
- additional Zebra crossings

Ten families would like to see less development (particularly regretting the demise of Melton Woods) and eight families would like the environment improved in some way. Three families requested cleaner pavements. Many people said that some use should be made of St Audry's Hospital and the Phyllis Memorial Home.

One person felt that the village did not have a 'centre'. Two other families would like more functions at church and more activities in the village. Three families would like better recreation facilities at the playing field and at least one villager would like a new parish hall. One family asked for a better train service and another for more light industrial work to be brought to the village. Finally, one family requested a resident policeman who could be seen regularly to be on foot patrol.

Forty per cent of the respondents said they belonged to either a club or a society and thirty seven per cent attended church regularly. Three quarters of the families felt they were part of the Melton community. There were no distinguishing factors to indicate whether or not a family felt part of Melton.

Six families had children at school in Melton. Four families had children that had grown up and stayed in Melton. Four pensioner families had attended school in Melton and one family had all been to school in Melton and their child was now at Melton School.

Fourteen families had one or more members working in Melton. Judging by their occupations, it appears that half are married women. The list of occupations is given below:

Consultant working from home
Sheet metal worker
Electronics - Dock Lane
Medical Osteopath
Nursery worker
Auto-electrician
Clerical Assistant
Dinner lady
Home carer
Ancillary helper
Cleaner

Thirty-two people felt they had something of interest to offer; these included photos of events in Melton, letters giving historic detail and background to the village and many related specific changes to the village. One gentleman related a past misdeed which is given overleaf:

"I remember back in the 60s when I was much younger climbing over the gate late one night and pinching some apples from a tree. Little did I realise that many years later myself and my family would be living not many yards from where I collected my 'ill gotten gains'. Back in those days much of Bury Hill was orchard and being close to Woods Lane was very tempting for a young chap with an appetite. I often think of that as I walk round Bury Hill all these years later."

Jefferson's Research
Easingwold
North Yorkshire.

March 1994.

## Significant oral input

Many Meltonians, particularly older residents, were happy to talk, often reminiscing about village events and personalities from the past. But criticism of the present community and its leaders, as one would expect, was far more muted ... "I would not like to be quoted" ... "I will give you my personal views but only in confidence" ... and so on. These revelations appeared to Robert Blake to be of varying significance, but to those sharing them they were of importance. Thus, much of the following may appear to be parochial but, as co-ordinator, I have included each with a minimum of reduction and editing.

A salient fact that became clear was that for many it was easier to talk direct rather than answer the questionnaire. We were surprised, as the object of the questionnaire survey had been to give anonymity and allow utmost confidence in expressing views, particularly those which could be controversial or personal. We received telephone calls from a number of parishioners who obviously preferred to talk directly and this has been further emphasised by some face to face encounters in the street or other public places. In many instances private and personal aspects of Melton life (both past and present) were happily divulged. With hindsight perhaps the questionnaire was not the best medium for carrying out this type of investigation.

Much of the information received by telephone and apparent chance encounters has been included in relevant sections of this book, and others stand on their own as vignettes. I have not been able to satisfy completely the question of how to include views expressed orally. If we include them in the figures given in the questionnaire this will skew the findings. However, as a compromise I draw attention as follows (not necessarily in order of priority):

a   A general recurring theme expressed by over eighty per cent of those who have spoken to me has been the need to restrict any further housebuilding within the village boundaries. The controversy over the fate of Melton Woods has served to draw attention to this underlying concern.

b   The inadequacy of the present parish room to meet the needs of the twenty-first century. Many younger people have expressed concern about the lack of facilities provided. Car-parking is another issue. At least six residents (two in the street area) have drawn attention to this need. Some residents have wistfully made comparisons between Melton Parish Room and newer halls/community centres in neighbouring villages, in particular Bredfield and Tunstall.

c   Improved retail outlets – this is of especial concern to older residents, who are concerned about the lack of choice from the two Melton shops and reminisce about times when Melton had a range of grocers' shops, bakers, butchers and other specialised trades. However, both present-day shop-keepers (as those in the past) are restricted to what is viable and the dictum remains: "Use it or lose it". In this context concern over public transport provision is equally pertinent.

d   Social provision within Melton: as with the previous issue, much depends upon local demand, organisation and leadership. The necessity for the community to meet its own needs is relevant. The Parish Council, P C C, Chapel, Old Church Society, etc., can only offer support and guidance. Issues, be they Church Services, street lighting, pavements, footpath maintenance – to name but four – need voicing to the right agency concerned. This is grassroots democracy. The means are there if only they are utilised.

# Conclusion

In virtually every way Melton has changed from what it was forty years ago. The increase in housing is immediately visible. Throughout the post-war period major housing estates have been constructed, commencing with Hall Farm Road in the late 1940s, St. Andrew's Place from the mid-50s, followed in steady succession by Bury Hill, River View, Melton Grange and so on. At times, particularly in the 1970s and early part of the '80s, major development was under way at more than one site within the village boundaries. Surprisingly, in view of so much building, there remain many open spaces, perhaps most clearly visible in the aerial photographs. This is confirmed at ground level when walking the parish, particularly from high vantage points like Leeks Hills. Further expansion is contained by the Deben on the East, Woodbridge town on the South and the A12 on the West and North. The next possible contentious area for development, now that the completion of building houses in Melton Woods is a virtual foregone conclusion, is likely to be at St. Audry's. The whole complex – buildings and land – has been on the market since its closure as a hospital. Opponents claim that any change of use will adversely affect the whole character of Melton and its environs. It is however salient to record that for over a century St. Audry's was a major employer, and in addition offered sanctuary to many hundreds (1,200+ in the 1950s) of residential patients at any one time. This is now all history, but any development within the boundaries of the former asylum must have beneficial 'spin-offs' for Melton itself.

The remnants of self-sufficiency, with trades and services providing for Meltonians' needs, have gone. The inter-relationship with the region as a whole is made possible by improved personal mobility and communications (of particular importance has been the telephone – more than 90% of Melton residents have their own telephones). Children and young people identify not exclusively with the place where they live (or possibly receive their education), but with the larger area. This is confirmed by the child who gave his home base as synonymous with his postcode. We all travel more, and over larger distances, both for work and recreation; and this is reflected in attitudes to our home community.

Development and change on all fronts, particularly the increase in housing and consequently Melton's population, are clearly seen when examining the 1986 'Domesday Survey' (which was carried out by the village recorder at the request of Suffolk History Council). Appendix 4 shows the major changes which have taken place over the last 8 years and which most dramatically affect the whole fabric of the village.

At times of need, be it a local event such as a fête, or the exhibition and launch of this book, the whole village will rally both in attending (and spending money to raise funds) but also to help organise. However, a large percentage of those involved will not live within the parish boundaries. The proposal in the late 1970s to sell off Melton's Old Church united the whole community, but again, considerable support came from outside.

Serious consideration has been given to the current role of St. Andrew's Church, which is very active and attracts a much higher than average regular attendance from all age groups. However, many worshippers live outside Melton. This is probably not only a reflection of the popularity of the present incumbent but also because of the range of Sunday Church Services on offer.

Melton County Primary School is another institution which is vibrant and alive (its pupils have increased from in 175 in 1986 to 205 in 1994); again, a large percentage come in from outside the village. This has obviously helped to broaden the ambience of the school, which in the 1950s and '60s would have been more parochial.

Many residents on the Woodbridge side of Melton look to the town both for work and recreation. In such cases, living in Melton is virtually restricted to using the postcode. Certainly, those residents living nearer to the village centre (a rough triangle of School, Street, St. Andrew's Church, and Wilford Bridge Road) tend to identify with a more traditional attitude to village life. Retail businesses, the Post Office Stores, Skouldings and the Fish and Chip Shop – all flourish preponderantly with support from Meltonians.

**Riverside view, north of Wilford Bridge, 1900 – photograph taken by the author's grandfather**

Employers are no longer restricted as in the last century to three or four major enterprises but now are far greater in number and more diverse in the range of products and services provided. However, the turnover of businesses is clearly seen when comparing the 1986 survey with that eight years later. Added to this, employees predominantly live outside the parish boundaries (of the 130 employees of Girdlestones, fewer than 20% live in Melton). Greater mobility for all ages and income groups within the U.K. as a whole is one of the most remarkable developments in the post-war period. For isolated communities there will be a stronger tendency to be more self-sufficient in all respects, but for Meltonians and those living in similar communities, the accessibility to neighbourhood means less dependence upon traditional ties.

**Riverside view, north of Wilford Bridge, 1994**

Melton, while it does not compete with the tourist attractions of Woodbridge, regrets its loss of some former amenities, has nevertheless beauties which repay the discerning, searching eye. One resident recently commented:

"To appreciate Melton one must have a vested interest".

*I believe there is more to Melton than this.*

117    **At Decoy Farm, early 20th century photograph**

# *Appendix 1*

## *Melton Directory*

*Melton Parish Council has published this leaflet to provide brief infor-*
*mation about current local government organisation, some local*
*amenities and organisations, and the persons to contact. (The Melton*
*Directory is updated regularly for publication, and circulated to every*
*household in Melton.)*

### 1   MELTON PARISH COUNCIL

The Parish Council represents you at the most local level of government. The Council voices the views of Melton residents and
acts on their behalf on a wide range of issues that affect the
Parish. The Council is asked by the District Council for its views
on all planning applications within the parish, whilst the Parish
Council has many duties and functions in its own right. It owns
Melton Playing Field and part of the adjacent woodland, together with the Pavilion, Tennis Courts and children's play equipment on the grounds. The Council is always eager to take a lead
on issues affecting the interests of the area and its residents, so if
there is a local issue that *YOU* are concerned about contact any
one of the following Councillors: *Full list of Councillors*

Parish Council meetings are normally held at the Parish Room in
The Street at 7.30 p.m. on the second Wednesday in alternate
months, viz. January, March, May, July, September and
November. The March meeting is preceded by the Annual
Parish Meeting.

The meetings are open to the public – details, dates and times are
posted on the Parish Council notice board, or can be obtained
from the Clerk to the Council (Name, address and telephone
number given), to whom enquiries relating to any Parish Council
business may also be addressed.

*The Parish Council is there to assist Melton residents – don't hesitate*
*to let us know if you have, or know of, a local problem.*

(Name, address and telephone number of Parish Recorder given)
would welcome information and memorabilia of Melton and district, both past and present, e.g. postcards and photographs.

### 2   SUFFOLK COASTAL DISTRICT COUNCIL
(address and telephone number given)

Name of District Council Representative for Melton given.
She may be able to help.

### 3   SUFFOLK COUNTY COUNCIL
(address and telephone number given)

Brief list of responsibilities and relationship with Melton.

Your County Council Representative for Melton given together
with address and tel. no. If you are unhappy with any aspect of
the County Council operations in Melton and cannot resolve it
direct with County Hall, let Mrs. Cowper know – she will be
pleased to try to help.

### 4   RECREATION IN MELTON

The Playing Field consists of general playing areas for recreation
with marked football pitches, practice areas and Pavilion hired by
Melton Sports and Social Club and Woodbridge Youths F.C.
There is play equipment for children on the Field, swings, see-
saw, roundabout, and climbing frame.

Vandalism to the pavilion and play equipment is a real problem
and is costing you, the Melton tax-payer, money. If you see anything suspicious ring the police (Woodbridge 383377).

If you are exercising your dog on the Playing Field, please remember the safety of children and keep your pet under control at all times. To avoid health risks, dogs must be prevented from fouling on the recreation areas. There is a 'fido bin' near the main entrance to the Field.

Unauthorised games, sports or events which may be dangerous to the public, such as playing golf, are not allowed. Similarly, horses and ponies are not permitted on the Playing Field. The Parish Council cannot accept responsibility for accidents.

There are two Tennis Courts on the Playing Field available for hire. If you or your family wish to play, you can book a court by contacting Skoulding's Newsagents, The Street, Melton.

In the Parish Council's area of mixed woodland adjacent to the playing field, since the Great Storm of 1987, over 1,000 trees have been re-planted. There is a public footpath through the woods, from Leeks Hill Road to Turnpike Lane.

A picnic and amenity area near the railway station at Wilford Bridge Road, with a duck pond, is run by the District Council. Footpaths join the river wall footpath which leads to Woodbridge.

## 5    SOME ORGANISATIONS AND CLUBS IN MELTON AND WHO TO CONTACT

*Burness Parish Room, The Street:*
Available for hire – name of secretary, treasurer and chairman given.

*Melton Old Church, Old Church Road:*
Occasional exhibitions, concerts and seasonal activities. Available to other organisations for hire. Contact name of chairman given.

*Melton Sports and Social Club:*
Two football teams operate under the auspices of M.S.S.C.

*Melton United:*
contacts given.

*Woodbridge Youths Football Club:*
Contacts given.

*Melton Bowls Club, Dock Lane:*
Secretary listed.

*1st Melton Brownie Pack:*
Meet on Tuesdays in the Parish Room. Contact listed.

*1st Melton Guide Company:*
Meet on Fridays in the Parish Room. Contact listed.

*Village Produce Association:*
Contact listed.

*Woodbridge Flower Club:*
Meets in the Parish Room. Contact listed.

*Hard of Hearing Group:*
Meets in the Parish Room. Contact listed.

*Woodbridge Open Door Club:*
Meets alternate Thursdays in the Parish Room. Contact listed.

*Civil Service Retirement Fellowship:*
Contact listed.

*Melton Trust Charity:*
Information can be obtained from clerk/treasurer. Contact listed.

6    THE CHURCH AND CHAPEL IN MELTON

*St. Andrew's Church, Station Road:*
Rector:  Rev. Mark Sanders
Deacon:  Rev. Clare Sanders  Melton Rectory.

*Melton Chapel, The Street:*
Pastor's name and address listed.


7    EDUCATION

*Melton Under-fives Playgroup:*
Contact listed.

*Melton Nursery School:*
At the Parish Room, The Street (a.m. only). Contact listed.

*Old Rectory Montessori School:*
For 3 to 6 years olds. Contact listed.

*Melton Primary School, Melton Road:*
Headmaster listed (telephone number).


8    SHELTERED HOUSING

*Suffolk Heritage Housing Association:*
The Grove, Pytches Road.  Warden's tel. no. given.
Winifred Fison House, The Street.  Warden's tel. no. given.


9    PUBLIC TRANSPORT

*Buses:*
Main services pass through Melton Street.

*Railway:*
All trains stop at Melton Station.

# Appendix 2

## Questionnaire

Blakes Agricultural Engineers (Melton) Ltd.
Station Road
Melton
Woodbridge
IP12 1PX

Tel: 0423 525760

November 1993

Dear Parishioner,

Currently I am carrying out research into the history and present day life of Melton. As part of the project I am writing to each household. We need your help. Please spare us some of your time by completing this questionnaire and returning it to me at Station Road or to one of the collection points listed on the back.

I am anxious to hear stories and anecdotes relating to organisations, events and people living in Melton now, and in the past. I would appreciate seeing photographs and/or objects and learning of other things, with a local interest, which might be used in a book to be published in 1994.

If I use your material you may choose whether your contribution is acknowledged in the book or you may wish to remain anonymous. Items of interest can be photographed in your home, thus ensuring no loss or damage.

For this project to be useful it will be helpful if all the questionnaires are returned to us even though you may feel that the questions do not relate to your circumstances. Your responses will be professionally analysed and reported in the book. Although some of the questions are personal please note that I only require your name if you want me to contact you and your anonymity is assured.

Thank you for your help. The book will be launched locally in September 1994 and available at good bookshops.

Yours faithfully,

Robert Blake

# Questionnaire

1.  How long have you lived in Melton?

2.  What changes, if any, would you like to see to Melton?

3.  Do you or any member of your family belong to Melton clubs or societies?

4.  Do you or any member of your family regularly attend a religious service in Melton?

5.  Do you feel that you and your family are part of the Melton Community?

6.  Age of each member living in your home:

    Under 16        16-39           40-64           65-75           80+

Male:

Female:

7.  How many of the above attended or presently attend Melton School?

8.  If any member of your family works in Melton, please give their occupations.

9.  Please tell us anything that you feel is of interest. If necessary continue onto the back page.

*Thank you for your help.*

# Appendix 3

## Shops and Service in Melton – 1874

*Taken from White's 1874 Suffolk Directory*

Anderson, William Hennessy – Saddler and Harness maker

Ball, William – Butcher

Bennington and Branwhite – Corn, Coal, Seed, Cake and Guano Merchants and Maltsters

Bilby, William – Joiner, Bricklayer, Builder, Plumber and Glazier (Shop and premises opposted St. Andrew's New Church)

Booth, George – Tailor

Chaplin, William – Blacksmith

Culpitt, John – Wheelwright

Dunnett, William – Grocer and Pork Butcher

Fisher, George – Corn Chandler and Boot and Shoe Maker

Fisher, Robert Bilby – Hay and Straw Dealer

Franklin, Thomas – Horse Slaughterer and Grease Manufacturer

Loder, Junior – Bookseller

Mallett, Joseph – Brewer's Agent and Victualler, Coach and Horses

Mannall, William – Baker and Coal Dealer

Manning, George – Shopkeeper

Page and Girling – Iron Founders and Machine Makers

Sawyer, James – Baker, Brewer and Beer Retailer

Skoulding, Alfred William – Grocer, Draper and Postmaster

Spalding, Frederick – Corn, Coal, Coke, Lime, Cement, Brick and Tile Merchant at new quay

Welton – Shoemaker.

# *Appendix* 4

### 1986 *Domesday Survey compared with available information for* 1994

| *1986* | *1994* |
|---|---|
| 1   *Population:*  3,009 | *4,508* |
| 2   *Number of houses:*  1.073 | *1,400* |

3   *Names and types of shops:*

| | |
|---|---|
| Antique shop at old Brewery next to Coach and Horses | *Antique shop* |
| Melton Antiques, Melton Road | *Melton Antiques* |
| Grocery stores:  N.P. Hutt, The Street. Off-licence. | *N.P. Hutt* |
| B. Skoulding, Newsagent and groceries, The Street (Estab. 1855) | *B. Skoulding* |
| "The Fruit Bowl", Greengrocers, The Street | *Now closed* |
| "The Golden Grenadier", Fish and Chips | *Now with new owner* |
| Foys shop (late Friars Pork Butchers), The Street | *Now closed* |

4   *Names of Public Houses:*

The Coach and Horses
The Horse snd Groom
The Wilford Inn
Melton Grange Hotel

5   *Names and types of Services and Businesses:*

| | |
|---|---|
| Girdlestone Mouldings Ltd., Melton Hill | *Now closed* |
| Fairhead and Sawyer, Melton Rd., Garage services. (Est 1920) | |
| John Riches Ltd., Agricultural Engineers 1973 | |
|    (On site of Page & Girling, Iron foundry 1839-1930) | *Now Thurlows* |
| Phoenix Labels, Printing Firm | |
| The Forge, Mr. Blake | |
| Technicraft Anglia Ltd., Wilford Bridge Road | |

## *1986*

## *1994*

Girdlestone Pumps Ltd.

W. Carter, Haulage, Ltd. (Est. 1928)  *CEL & Associates*

Micklewright, Coal & Coke, Station Office.  *New Charrington's site in Old Station Yard*

S.A. Nunn  Builder, Station Road

Anglian Quality Fuels Ltd., Melton Hill  *Now closed*

Blyth Hasel, Removals, Storage, Shipping, Melton Road  *Now closed*

Boat Yard, Ltd., Mel Skeet, Dock Lane

Boat Yard, Dick Larkman, Dock Lane

Hypoguard Ltd., Dock Lane

Cogent Technology

Anglia Grain Installations Ltd., Dock Lane  *Now closed*

Kent Blaxill, Paint & Glass, Wilford Bridge Spur

Overseas Sales (UK) Ltd., Taxfree Car Specialists, Wilford Bridge Spur  *Now closed*

Melton Tyre & Exhaust Centre, Wilford Bridge Spur

Mazda Garneys & Hill, Wilford Bridge Spur  *Now closed*

Deben Electronics Ltd., Wilford Bridge Road

C.E.L. Group Ltd., Wilford Bridge Road

H & R Block, Income Tax Consultants, Station Office  *Now closed*

Melwood Car Hire & Taxi, Station Office

Micklewright Tar Macadam Ltd., Station Office  *Now closed*

R & B Clarke, Lawn Mower Sales and Repairs, Church Close

Gold Star Construction, Building Firm, Melton Road

Morgan Cosmetics, Saddlemakers Lane  *Now closed*

John Barry, Ladies & Gents Hair Stylist, The Street  *Now "Rough Cuts"*

Michael R. Ashton, Building Design Consultants Agency, The Street  *Now closed*

Andrews Dixon, Builders, Agency, The Street  *Now closed*

W. Bloss, Haulage Contractor, The Street

J.P. Clarke, Slaughter House, Valley Farm Road  *Now closed*

R. Eagle, Painter & Decorator, Chimney Sweep, Hall Farm Road

Suffolk County Council Dept. East Area, Dock Lane

Anglia Water Authority Norfolk & Suffolk Division, Southern Area Office
    Water Tower & Pump House, Bredfield Road

Stewart Clay Traps Ltd., Wilford Bridge Spur  *Now closed*

7   *Post Office:*

A sub-post office in the grocery stores and off-licence of N. Hutt

## *1986*                                              *1994*

8   *Doctor/Surgery:*

   Nearest Surgeries in Woodbridge
   Phyllis Memorial Maternity Home                    *Now closed*
   St Audry's Hospital                                *Now closed*
   Chiropodist Clinic, The Street


9   *Places of Worship:*

   St. Andrew's Parish Church (C of E) built 1868:
      Overall average Sunday attendance: 70           *Now 180-200*
      (Melton Old Church, 12th C, made redundant 1978, in the care of the
      Old Church Society, formed 1981, Christian, community & educational uses
      occasional Service authorised by the Bishop)
   Melton Evangelical Church F.I.E.C. (Melton Chapel, built 1860)
      2 services on Sunday, one mid-week, average weekly attendance: 40
   Avenue Evangelical Church F.I.E.C. (covers boundary with Woodbridge)
      3 services on Sunday, one mid-week, average weekly attendance: 35
      Active teenage Youth Club 35 members.
   Christian Servicemen's Centre, Pentecostal, for U.S. personnel
      Sunday Worship Service, Family Bible Study       *Now closed*


10  *Schools:*

   Melton County Primsry School. 160 children on register.     *Now 208*
   Numbers rise each term from new Estates.
   Kindergsrten, and a pre-school Playgroup


11  *Public Rooms:*

   Parish Hall, built 1904. Accommodates 100
   St Andrew's Church room

## 1986

## 1994

12  *Sporting Facilities:*

Recreation Ground:  Football, cricket. Swings and slides
Tennis Courts, 2
Bowling Green
Melton Riverside Picnic site, birdwatching facilities


13  *Public amenities:*
Telephone Kiosk. St Andrew's Place and The Street, near sub-post office.
Post Box, Melton Road, St Andrew's Place, Bredfield Road
Police house                                                         *Now sold*
Electricity sub-station
Sewage farm
Anglia Water, Norfolk and Suffolk River Division, Southern Area Office,     *New reservoir and enlarged pump-house*
        Water Tower and pump house, Bredfield Road

14  *Bus services:*

Ipswich to Stradbroke, weekly – 21
Stradbroke to Ipswich, weekly – 29     All pass through Melton          *Bus services reduced*
Ipswich to Aldeburgh, weekly – 20
Aldeburgh to Ipswich, weekly – 18


14a *British Rail:*

Melton Station re-opened 1984 after 30 years closure
Liverpool St to Lowestoft – Weekly 15, Sunday 3 each way, stop at Melton     *Service reduced*
Lowestoft to Liverpool St – Weekly 17


15  *Special Accommodation for the Elderly:*

Melton Grove, Pytches Road – 32
Winifred Fison House, Melton Street – 30

## 1986

## 1994

16  *Houses provided by Local Authority:*

Churchmans Close  29
Hall Farm Road    58
St Andrew's Place  98
St Andrew's Close  18
Woods Lane        11
Yarmouth Road      8

*Large percentage now home ownership*

17  *Local Clubs, Organisations:*

Melton Women's Institute
Young Farmers' Club
Melton Old Church Society
Melton & Bromeswell Conservative Ass.
Brownies
Guides
British Association of the Hard of Hearing
Village Produce Association
Boy Scouts

18  *Farms:*

| | | |
|---|---|---|
| Witchpit Farm: | 100 acres. Part Melton part Bredfield | |
| Decoy Farm: | 105 acres + 20 leased from Hall Aggregates (late Ellinger's Farm) Farmer – Mr Bye | |
| Spring Farm: | 9 acres. Mr Steel | |
| Valley Farm: | Mr Arthur Bloss | |
| Lodge Farm: | 130 acres. The Misses Churchman, farmed by Mr William Warburg. 100 acres arable, the rest parkland and woods. Wheat, rape, barley and rye. | *Misses Churchman deceased* |
| The Old Mill: | Mr Keith Sangster (Thompson & Morgan) 25 acres let to Mr Flemming (farmer from Eyke) for grazing | *Increased acreage cultivated by Mr. Sangster* |
| Foxboro' Hall: | 100 acres farmed by Mr Rolph, Grove Farm, Ufford Suffolk Wildlife Trust, Foxborrow Farm Field Centre (off Saddlemaker's Lane) | *Increasing activity and visitors to area* |

*1986*                                              *1994*
_____                 _____

19  *Other information:*

The Village of Melton is changing rapidly;  the building of houses,        *Contentious point of book!*
the destruction of woodland and open spaces will soon make it become
a suburb of Woodbridge

Residents fear the loss of the Village identity.


Village Recorder:      Name and Address:

Mrs R.F. Blake
1a Moorfield Road
Woodbridge
 IP12 4JN

Tel: Woodbridge 382565

# Appendix 5

*St. Audry's staffing and patient figures 1929 - 1986*

| Year | Patients M | F | Total | Nurses home | E/house W/house Lodges | S/Close | U.M.T. | Staff total | Approx. Nursing | Other |
|------|------|------|-------|-------------|------------------------|---------|--------|-------------|-----------------|-------|
| 1829 | 40 | 73 | 113 | | | | – | 18 | 10 | 8 |
| 1844 | 195 | 135 | 330 | | | | – | 35 | 20 | 15 |
| 1874 | 200 | 250 | 450 | | | | – | 50 | 30 | 20 |
| 1902 | 400 | 500 | 900 | | | | – | 114 | 75 | 39 |
| 1938 | 550 | 650 | 1200 | 60 | 6 | – | 12 | 200 | 132 | 68 |
| 1948 | 500 | 600 | 1100 | 60 | 6 | – | 12 | 280 | 190 | 90 |
| 1959 | 450 | 550 | 1000 | 50 | 6 | 8 | 12 | 300 | 195 | 105 |
| 1980 | 230 | 270 | 500 | 20 | 4 | 8 | 12* | 613 | 400 | 213 |
| 1986 | 175 | 205 | 380 | Nil | 3 | 8 | 12 | 500 | 330 | 170 |

*Note: "Staff resident" spans the columns Nurses home, E/house W/house Lodges, S/Close, and U.M.T.*

* See next page

| | 1980 | Staff resident | | | |
|---|---|---|---|---|---|
| | | W/lodge | E/lodge | U.M.T. | S/Close |
| Nursing: Male | 175 | | | 8 | 4 |
| Female | 225 | | | | |
| Admin/Medical | 20 | 1 | | | 2 |
| Laundry | 10 | | | | |
| Gardens | 5 | | | | |
| Kitchens | 20 | | 1 | | |
| Day Hospital/CSSD/Occ. Therapy | 20 | | | | |
| Engineers/Stockers | 15 | | | 4 | 2 |
| Carpenters etc. | 29 | | | | |
| Domestics | 50 | | | | |
| General Porters | 15 | | | | |
| Transport Drivers | 10 | | | | |
| Refuse | 3 | | | | |
| Stores | 3 | | | | |
| Other Ancilliary | 22 | | | | |

Total     613

**Extracting gravel north of Wilford Bridge, 1991**

**1993, Fishing lakes on same site**

**1845 Davy engraving**